"In *Grace for the Children,* scientifically sound overvie children. This book provides important scientific information, practical advice, and a thoughtful theological perspective on disorders such as depression, ADHD, PTSD, and eating disorders. It is an extremely helpful resource for parents and other adults seeking to understand and support youth who struggle with these symptoms."

Sarah E. Hall, associate professor of psychology, Wheaton College

"Written by a Christian psychologist who knows his clients and his readership, *Grace for the Children* is a much-needed resource for parents, teachers, children's pastors, and youth workers who may be dealing with the behavioral and emotional challenges of children and adolescents who struggle with mental illness. The case examples that begin and end each chapter provide a realistic sense of what each disorder looks like and the difficulties involved in finding out what works for a particular child, as well as offering hope that symptoms can improve. The research findings related to the risk factors, neurobiology, and treatment of each disorder are well documented and are summarized in a way that will be easily comprehended by the lay reader. Finally, the biblical examples that are woven throughout offer a very helpful spiritual framework for how to view mental illness in children and youth."

Heather Davediuk Gingrich, professor of counseling at Denver Seminary, author of *Restoring the Shattered Self*

"*Grace for the Children* by Dr. Matthew Stanford is an excellent and comprehensive clinical guide for finding hope in the midst of child and adolescent mental illness. It covers autism spectrum disorder, ADHD, disruptive behavior disorders, depressive disorders, bipolar disorders, anxiety disorders, PTSD, OCD and related disorders, and eating disorders. It also includes helpful spiritual and biblical perspectives. Highly recommended!"

Siang-Yang Tan, professor of psychology, Fuller Theological Seminary, senior pastor, First Evangelical Church Glendale, California, author of *Counseling and Psychotherapy*

"This book offers help that is not only expert but also wise, realistic, practical, and specific. In its pages, Dr. Stanford will meet you where you are and point you toward both guidance and grace. For families affected by mental illness, it's a much-needed lifeline. For church leaders serious about the divine opportunity before us, it's an invaluable resource."

Amy Simpson, author of *Troubled Minds: Mental Illness and the Church's Mission*

"I'm thankful for Matt Stanford's heart for the hurting. In *Grace for the Children*, he shows us a path forward to meeting the needs of children and families affected by mental illness. With a deep knowledge of the field and a solid Christian commitment, *Grace for the Children* will bring the hope, encouragement, and direction you need."

Ed Stetzer, Billy Graham Professor of Church, Mission, and Evangelism, Wheaton College

"Here is the most helpful guide available for Christian parents (and ministers) who want information about childhood and adolescent psychological disorders. Written from a strong faith perspective by an experienced clinical psychologist and researcher committed to Christ and the church, this accessible, compassionate introduction to the major mental and emotional problems that can afflict children and teens wisely addresses the kinds of concerns caregivers have when faced with such difficulties."

Eric L. Johnson, professor of Christian psychology, Houston Baptist University

"The topic of mental illness is almost taboo in far too many churches today, yet hurting people sit in our pews. There is nothing more frightening to a parent than to watch a child struggle with mental illness, causing out-of-control behavior, mood swings, and public embarrassment. In *Grace for the Children*, Dr. Matthew Stanford encourages parents while educating the church on how to love and minister to children and teens with mental illness. Through the pages of this grace-filled narrative, you will discover how to love these children as Jesus loves them. This book will go a long way in removing the stigma affixed to this topic and replacing it with Christlike compassion."

Janet Parshall, nationally syndicated talk show host

"With clarity and compassion, Dr. Matt Stanford provides a vital resource for parents, pastors, and clinicians who have a heart for children who struggle with mental illness. *Grace for the Children* explains clinical information that becomes understandable and applicable while also laying the biblical foundation for compassionate and intentional responding. Most importantly, Dr. Stanford has infused the book with grace and hope; it is aptly titled!"

David E. Jenkins, professor of counseling at Liberty University

"This is a book every parent and pastor needs to read! Dr. Matthew Stanford defines mental illness in children and adolescents, and explains its causes, effects, and possible treatments in easy-to-understand language. The format is not only clear and concise but full of deep compassion for the children who suffer and for those who love them."

Kay Warren, cofounder of Saddleback Church

grace for the children

FINDING HOPE IN THE MIDST OF CHILD AND ADOLESCENT MENTAL ILLNESS

Matthew S. Stanford

An imprint of InterVarsity Press
Downers Grove, Illinois

InterVarsity Press
P.O. Box 1400, Downers Grove, IL 60515-1426
ivpress.com
email@ivpress.com

InterVarsity Press® is the book-publishing division of InterVarsity Christian Fellowship/USA®, a movement of students and faculty active on campus at hundreds of universities, colleges, and schools of nursing in the United States of America, and a member movement of the International Fellowship of Evangelical Students. For information about local and regional activities, visit intervarsity.org.

While any stories in this book are true, some names and identifying information may have been changed to protect the privacy of individuals.

Significant parts of this book have been published previously on the Mental Health Gateway website (mentalhealthgateway.org) of which Matthew S. Stanford is the CEO; Mental Health Grace Alliance (mentalhealthgracealliance.org), of which Matthew S. Stanford is a cofounder; and Matthew S. Stanford's blog, "Mindful of Grace" (mindfulofgrace.blogspot.com). Used with permission.

Cover design and image composite: Cindy Kiple
Interior design: Jeanna Wiggins
Images: girl running: © Mary Wethey / Trevillion Images
girl running: © Mark Owen / Trevillion Images
mother and child hands: © Milkos / iStock / Getty Images Plus

ISBN 978-0-8308-4576-7 (print)
ISBN 978-0-8308-5791-3 (digital)

Printed in the United States of America ♾

InterVarsity Press is committed to ecological stewardship and to the conservation of natural resources in all our operations. This book was printed using sustainably sourced paper.

Library of Congress Cataloging-in-Publication Data
A catalog record for this book is available from the Library of Congress.

P	17	16	15	14	13	12	11	10	9	8	7	6	5	4	3	2	1
Y	33	32	31	30	29	28	27	26	25	24	23	22	21	20	19		

Contents

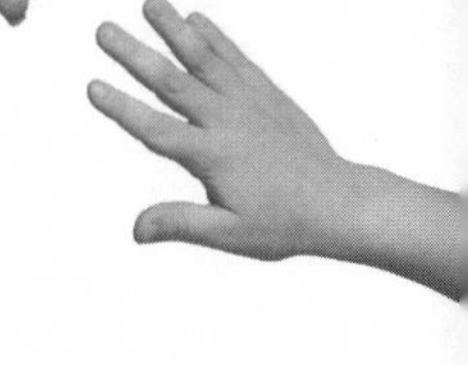

1

A Gift and a Reward

Behold, children are a gift of the LORD,
the fruit of the womb is a reward.

PSALM 127:3

ONE OF MY PASSIONS is training pastors and ministry staff to recognize and respond to the mental-health problems of those they are serving. At the end of my workshops, we always have a question and answer time, and during one of these sessions a young pastor raised her hand. She wanted to know the best way to minister to a new family that had recently started attending her church.

Ross, Ellen, and their two children, Ashley and Charlie, moved to the area three years ago. At that time Charlie had just turned five and was beginning kindergarten while Ashley was going into the second grade. The family was interested in attending a small Bible church near their home, so Ellen made an appointment with the children's minister to discuss

Charlie. In the year prior to their move Charlie had been diagnosed with mild autism, and while he was a happy, carefree little boy he did have trouble sitting still and tended to wander. The children's minister assured Ellen that the Sunday school staff could accommodate Charlie, and he was welcomed with open arms.

Most Sunday mornings that first year Charlie did fine, but at least once a month one of his parents had to be called out of the service to get him. At school the academic and behavioral demands of kindergarten were simply too much for Charlie, and he quickly fell behind. Frustrated, he began acting out. By the middle of the year he had been moved to a special education class. Over the next two years Charlie's behavior on Sunday mornings deteriorated. He would pace around the class and refuse to sit down. When frustrated he would yell and disrupt the class. His yelling was often so loud that he could be heard in the service. In first grade Charlie was given an additional diagnosis of Attentional Deficit Hyperactivity Disorder.

Many Sundays either Ellen or Ross would stay home with Charlie so the other parent could attend church with Ashley. Charlie's behavioral problems were taking a toll on the family. They felt isolated and alone. One Sunday morning Charlie bit his Sunday school teacher when she was trying to restrain him. Charlie was prescribed medication by a child psychiatrist to help control his impulsive behavior. On several occasions the children's minister met with Ellen and Ross, but it was clear that she considered Charlie the "bad kid" and saw his behavior the result of willful disobedience rather than a neuro-developmental disorder. The church's response to Charlie was more disciplinary than accommodating.

Things reached a head one Sunday morning when Charlie, now seven, threw a toy at another child, causing a large laceration on the girl's forehead. To remedy the problem, the church's leadership sought a restraining order against Charlie so that he could not attend. This was done without consulting Ellen and Ross, who found out about the restraining order when a constable delivered court documents to their home one afternoon. Now seriously wounded by the body of Christ, this broken family was seeking refuge at a new church. The twenty or so pastors in the room at my workshop were speechless.

How could anyone imagine that a restraining order against a suffering child and struggling family expresses the unconditional love and limitless grace of Christ? But this type of harmful response to mental illness is not uncommon in the church. My own research on Christians with mental illness demonstrates that 30-40 percent of them have had a negative interaction (such as having a pastor tell them there is no such thing as mental illness) when they seek counseling or assistance from their church in relation to their disorder.[1]

Mental illness is a terrifying experience, especially when a father and mother have to watch their child suffer from destructive, uncontrollable thoughts, feelings, and behaviors. Given Jesus' heart for children (Matthew 19:13-15; Mark

10:13-16; Luke 18:15-17), the church should be a place of grace and unconditional love for families struggling to care for a child with mental illness. Unfortunately, due to fear and spiritual ignorance, the church has struggled in ministering to these families. It is my hope that the information presented in this book will provide a better understanding of mental illness, both from a scientific perspective and through the eyes of faith. To truly minister to suffering children and their families the way that Christ would, we must see them with his eyes. So let's start by understanding God's creative role in the birth of all children.

THE HANDS OF THE MAKER

All children are "fearfully and wonderfully made" in the image of God (Genesis 1:26). A creative act similar to the creation of Adam is repeated at the origin of each person. God wills that each individual life comes into existence and actively sustains them moment by moment (Colossians 1:16-17). God knits all children together in their mothers' wombs (Psalm 139:13-16), and they are all—even those with developmental and psychological disorders—conceived for the purpose of displaying his glory (Isaiah 43:7). God is intentional in the creation of his children (Psalm 119:73), endowing each with a divine purpose and plan (Jeremiah 29:11) and bestowing them as a gift and reward upon their earthly parents (Psalm 127:3). Even before a child is conceived, God knows everything about them and longs for an intimate relationship with them (Psalm 139:16; Jeremiah 1:5; Ephesians 1:4-5). The Scriptures tell us that it is beyond our finite minds to fully grasp this divine process (Ecclesiastes 11:5), but we should rest in the fact that God is intentional and intimately involved in the creation of every new life.

Every newborn child is a highly complex being, unlike any other living creature God has made. The Scriptures tell us that we are an embodied spirit, having both physical (material) and nonphysical (immaterial) aspects to our being (1 Thessalonians 5:23). Describing the developing Christ child, Luke outlines four aspects to our being (Luke 2:52). He writes, "Jesus kept increasing in wisdom [mental] and stature [physical], and in favor with God [spiritual] and men [relational]." So a child, like the young incarnate Christ, is a unity of physical, mental, spiritual, and relational facets, with each aspect affecting and being affected by all the others.

Physical. All children are born into a physical world, and to interact with it, an aspect of their being must be physical. God has given them a complex set of sensory systems that allows them to take in stimulation from the environment and relay it to the brain. They can touch, taste, see, smell, and hear the world around them. At birth, however, a child's brain is not fully developed. A combination of inborn genetic information and experience shapes how their brain cells will develop and connect. These new connections form specialized systems that give rise to their thoughts, feelings, and emotions. This process of brain maturation is ongoing throughout childhood and adolescence, with the development of some neural systems not being fully complete until early adulthood.[2]

Our bodies are the aspect of our being that we are most aware of on a daily basis. Believers and nonbelievers alike, scientists, philosophers, and theologians all agree that we have a physical body. However, the Scriptures are clear: we are more than simply a physical body (2 Corinthians 5:8). There is an immaterial, nonphysical aspect to our being—what some would call our soul or mind.

Mental. Children's thoughts, feelings, and emotions are more than simply the product of neurochemical changes and electrical discharges in the brain. While the functioning of the brain is integral to the existence of the mind, that alone is not sufficient to explain it. Similarly, to imagine the mind as completely separate and unrelated to the physical doesn't seem correct either. The mind, what some might call consciousness or soul, is a bridge between the material and the immaterial. As an extension of the physical (brain) world, it allows a child to interact with the nonphysical (spirit). In the mind they plan actions (Proverbs 16:9), choose to sin or not to sin (Romans 8:6-7; 2 Corinthians 10:5), connect with God through prayer (1 Corinthians 14:15), receive divine revelation and understanding (Luke 24:45), meditate on the truths of God (Colossians 3:2), and are transformed by the indwelling of the Holy Spirit (Romans 12:2).

The mind of a child, while endowed with godly attributes (Matthew 18:2-4) at birth, is not fully developed, and much like the brain is shaped by a combination of genetics and experience as we grow (Proverbs 22:6,15; Luke 2:52; Colossians 3:21). The Scriptures teach us that we also have a third and even more amazing level of being, a spirit.

Spiritual. Like God himself, our children are spiritual beings: God has breathed his very breath into them (Genesis 2:7). That's how we differ from the animals: like the animals, we were created from the dust of the ground (Genesis 2:19), but only humans bear the breath of God: his very image. As spiritual beings, then, our children have the potential for an intimate spiritual union with God. No other living creature, not even the angels, is given such an opportunity.

Relational. Our children were also created to be in relationship. God himself said, "It is not good for the man to be alone" (Genesis 2:18). While our first and greatest relational need is to know God, we should never underestimate the importance of being in fellowship with other believers. The topic of relationship is common throughout the Scriptures. The Bible offers us guidance on a variety of relationships, including marriage (Ephesians 5:22-33), parenting (Psalm 127:3-5), siblings (Proverbs 17:17), friendships (Proverbs 27:9), and with those who are not so friendly (Matthew 5:25). Relationship is one of the reasons why Jesus gave us the church: so we might be together and never be alone (Acts 2:42; 1 John 1:7).

THE HOLISTIC SELF

So how does all this—physical, mental, spiritual, and relational—work together? Let's look at a simple visual representation I use with clients to help them understand how mental illness affects our whole being. Figure 1.1 shows the spiritual, mental, physical, and relational facets of our being, each separate but interacting with the others. Our physical body interacts with stimuli and individuals (relationships) in the environment outside and the mind within. The mind, connected to the body through the functions of the brain and nervous system, is also in contact with our immaterial spirit.

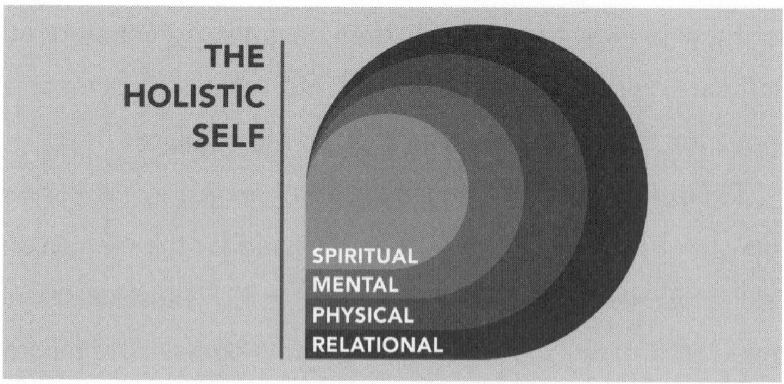

Figure 1.1. The holistic self

Our body senses and reacts to the external environment, and our mind uses that information to perceive, understand, and interpret our surroundings. The mind forms our thoughts and plans our actions. Our spirit, when connected to God, works to transform the mind into the image of Christ (2 Corinthians 3:18). This interaction within our being allows us to be involved in healthy, meaningful relationships with others.

Since we were created as a unity, dysfunction or disorder in one aspect of the self negatively affects all levels of our being. For example, in a child diagnosed with a mental illness, a neurochemical dysfunction in the brain (physical) results in abnormal thoughts and feelings (mental) leading to broken relationships (relational) and difficulty connecting with God and other believers (spiritual).

EFFECTS OF SIN ON THE PHYSICAL CREATION

If God is intimately involved in the creation of every new life, why are so many children born with developmental and psychological disorders? To answer this question, we have to go back to the parents of all humans, Adam and Eve. Created spiritually innocent and sinless, Adam and Eve knew an intimacy with God that we can only imagine (Genesis 3:8). They were in perfect harmony with their Creator and with one another (Genesis 2:25). He gave them life and provided for their every need. He was their daily companion, their friend, and he dearly loved them. In Eden all things were possible, and only a single behavior was forbidden; they were told never to eat the fruit from the tree of the knowledge of good and evil. If they did, God said that they would die (Genesis 2:17). Questioning the heart of God, Adam and Eve chose to sin, and everything changed. Instead of being in a harmonious, loving relationship with their Creator, they now feared him and hid (Genesis 3:8). Spiritually, they were separated from him. God removed his protective hand and cast them out of Eden, leaving them and their descendants at the mercy of unrestrained environmental and biological processes that would wreak havoc on their bodies and minds. Sin brought disorder, disease, and death into the world (Romans 5:12-14; 8:18-25).

At conception, we are all separated from God and physically damaged as a result of original sin (Psalm 51:5).[3] Our spiritual condition is identical; we are all dead in our sins, unable to know God. Physically, however, the effects of sin vary in our bodies from minor bodily annoyances to major debilitating abnormalities. Can this reality be reconciled with a good God who is intimately involved in the creation of each human being? God creates each individual, much like Adam and Eve, whole and complete, as he would have them be within his perfect will (Psalm 139:13-16). He also endows them with unique talents and gifts so they might fulfill their divine purpose (Jeremiah 29:11). God does not create disease or disorder within our bodies. The Scriptures tell us that the physical creation is damaged by sin and longs for the day of redemption (Romans 8:20-22). God, because he is just, allows the consequence of original sin to run its course, which results in the disorder, disease, and death we face here on earth. I'll be the first to say that I don't fully understand it all or why it is this way. However, I do know that recognizing how intimately God is involved in the creation of each child with a developmental or psychological disorder should transform the way they are seen and treated by those around them.

THE EYES OF CHRIST

A child with a developmental or psychological disorder is not some cosmic accident or mistake of nature. Some in the world may think of them that way, but God certainly doesn't. Sadly, even the church has struggled in ministering to these hurting children and their families.

In the Gospel of John, Jesus and a man disabled from birth have an interaction that gives us insight into not only how Jesus sees those struggling with a disorder but also how we should respond in the midst of suffering (John 9:1-3): "As He passed by, He saw a man blind from birth. And his disciples asked Him, 'Rabbi, who sinned, this man or his parents, that he would be born blind?'" Jesus' disciples assumed that sin was the cause of the man's blindness. In fact, as we can see from their question, they believed that the man may have sinned before he was born and brought this punishment upon himself. This was a common belief of the day; sin or unrighteousness brought punishment (e.g., sickness, poverty, a physical handicap) while righteous living brought health and prosperity. There is an ugly sense of self-righteousness in that theology. But what does Jesus say? "Jesus answered, '*It was* neither *that* this man sinned, nor his parents; but *it was* so that the works of God might be displayed in him.'" This outcast, this "cursed" man, this sinner was blind from birth so the works of God might be displayed in him? Jesus then shows us how grace is to be extended to those struggling with a disorder. First, he touched the man to relieve his physical suffering, and later, after the man was mocked, humiliated, and thrown out by the Pharisees (John 9:13-34), Jesus sought him out and revealed to the man that he is the Messiah (John 9:35-39). The man was transformed both physically and spiritually. Christ's call to the church is no different today.

We are to relieve physical and psychological suffering while revealing the unconditional love and limitless grace that is available through a personal relationship with Jesus. We must not allow a child or a family to be defined by a disorder. Instead, we need to see with spiritual eyes, with Christ's eyes. He sees these beloved children as bearers of the divine image, created for his glory. Every trial, every malady, every weakness is yet another opportunity for the works of God to be manifest in their lives (and ours) because God is sovereign over illness and disorder, even mental illnesses and disorders. For example, in my thirty years of working with those living with mental illness, I have met countless Christ-followers whose faith was challenged but strengthened by a mental-health crisis in their family. Many of those same individuals have gone on to become mental-health advocates, peer counselors, and therapists sharing the love of Christ by serving other families who are now walking the same difficult path.

GRIEVING AND GRACE

When parents realize that something is wrong, it can feel like a punch in the gut. All the hopes and dreams they had for their child seem lost. It is not uncommon for parents to go through a range of emotions from anger to guilt, from fear to joy. Some find themselves questioning their religious beliefs and feel angry with God, while others find that their faith is all they have left to sustain them. These thoughts and feelings are not wrong or sinful but are simply part of normal grieving. Grieving after loss is a God-ordained process that Jesus himself went through during his earthly ministry.

After learning of his cousin John's (the Baptist) death, the Scriptures tell us Jesus got into a boat and went off to a secluded place to be alone (Matthew 14:13). The crowds often followed Jesus, and after some time, Jesus returned to find the crowds waiting for him. Jesus was full of compassion and ministered to the sick and later miraculously fed at least five thousand people. Throughout the Bible, grieving is seen as an important process after loss. Learning about a child's mental disorder is cause for grieving. In a very real sense the child the parents had joyfully anticipated and imagined is lost. God knows they need time to properly grieve because through this process they will receive comfort, grow in intimacy with him, and continue on with their life transformed forever.

Grieving is a process with a number of stages: denial ("This can't be happening"); anger ("God, why did you let this happen?"); bargaining ("Heal my child and in return I will ____"); depression ("I can't go on anymore"); and acceptance ("I'm at peace with the circumstances"). Not everyone who is grieving goes through all these stages, nor do the stages necessarily occur in the order I have listed them. A parent does not have to go through each stage in order to be healed. Healing happens gradually; it can't be forced or hurried—and there is no normal timetable for grieving.

During the grieving process, it is important for us to remember that God is faithful and present in our pain (Job 33:13-28). We don't have to fully understand God's role in the situation, but we must simply recognize he is present. Be honest with him. If you're angry, tell him. He can take it. If you feel overwhelmed, cry out to your Father. Lean on fellow believers, not to fix you or the situation but to be a listening ear as you vent your pain and disappointment. Let them bring you comfort, encouragement, and practical advice. Let them rejoice with you in the victories! Remember, Jesus took time to grieve and afterward was compassionate to give to those who so desperately needed him. Give yourself the same grace so you might show compassion and recognize that God has great plans for you.

CALLED AND EQUIPPED

God places children with developmental and psychological disorders in our lives in accordance with his will and for a divine purpose. As believers in Christ, He has also equipped us with all the love, patience, and wisdom necessary to support and raise them (2 Thessalonians 3:5). At times that may seem impossible, but remember we have been transformed by the indwelling Spirit (2 Corinthians 5:17), and all things are possible through Christ (Philippians 4:13). This is an opportunity for you to grow closer to him! A child may have greater cognitive and physical needs than most children but has the same spiritual needs that everyone has, including you—intimacy with Christ. Parents have been given the honor of training this child in Christ. God has a great purpose and plan for all children's lives, just as he does for yours.

As a community of believers, we must not withdraw from or ignore childhood mental disorders but instead choose to face them with God's grace and wisdom. Christ said that they would know we are his disciples because of our love for one another (John 13:35). Where better for children, whether they have a mental disorder or not, to look for love and acceptance than the church? Where better for parents to go for support and comfort than the body of Christ? As a community of faith, our approach to mental disorders should be one of love and grace.

2

Diagnosis and Treatment

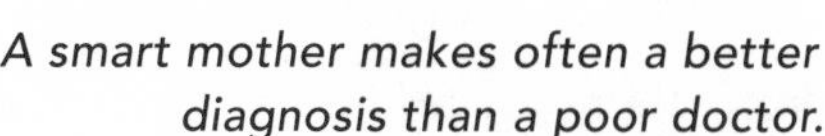

A smart mother makes often a better diagnosis than a poor doctor.

DR. AUGUST BIER

WHEN MY DAUGHTER WAS THREE or four years old, I was teaching a graduate neuroanatomy course at the university. For fun I taught her to name the four deep nuclei of the cerebellum: dentate, globose, emboliform, and fastigial. When asked, she could recite them perfectly, as if she fully understood what she was saying. I even once said to my graduate class, "This is so simple even my three year old knows it!"

We love precocious children; the three year old who reads at a high school level, the six-year-old piano virtuoso, the eight year old who shoots a 3 under par round of golf. We are drawn to these children because they support the long-held view that children are simply little adults who should think and act just like we do. These children, however, are exceptions, outliers who do not represent their peers.

When a child has a sore throat, we take them to a pediatrician because we understand that the medical needs of children differ from those of adults. The same is true for psychological disorders. The mental-health difficulties of children should be recognized as related to but clinically different from those of adults. A mental disorder in a child or adolescent is a serious change in the way they learn, behave, or handle their emotions, which causes distress and problems getting through the day. This change is significant enough that it requires treatment or intervention. While many children and adolescents will have significant changes in their thoughts, behaviors, and emotions during a normal childhood, those changes are not usually severe enough to require treatment or intervention. A mental disorder on the other hand is a debilitating experience in which the child is simply unable to function normally for his age over an extended period of time. Given this broad definition, one might wonder exactly how a child or adolescent is diagnosed with a specific mental disorder such as depression.

DIAGNOSIS

For the purposes of diagnosis and treatment, mental disorders have been categorized into groups according to their common symptoms in the *Diagnostic and Statistical Manual of Mental Disorders*, fifth edition (DSM-5), published by the

American Psychiatric Association. Within the DSM-5 there are nineteen primary diagnostic categories (e.g., neurodevelopmental disorders). Some categories contain large numbers of disorders, while others contain few. Within each category, the criteria are listed that must be present for a child or adolescent to be diagnosed with a specific mental disorder (e.g., obsessive-compulsive disorder). The decision by a mental-health professional to diagnose a child as suffering from a mental disorder is not a subjective one but rather is based on the presence of observable mood, behavioral, and cognitive criteria described in the DSM-5. The specific criteria for many of these disorders will be outlined in later chapters.

As with all medical conditions, an accurate diagnosis of a mental-health problem leads to more effective treatment. Three factors, however, make psychological diagnoses in children difficult. First, children, especially young children, lack the verbal and cognitive skills necessary to express how they are thinking and feeling. To overcome this problem and obtain diagnostic information, mental-health-care providers often rely on ratings from informants other than the child, such as teachers, parents, and day-care workers. Research has consistently shown that the ratings of social, emotional, and behavior problems in children from multiple informants often vary. These discrepancies between informants are the result of differing motivations for providing the ratings, differing thresholds or perceptions of what constitutes abnormal behavior in a given child, and the variability of children's behavior from one setting to the next (e.g., school versus home).[1]

The second factor that makes psychological diagnoses in children difficult is that many behaviors we recognize as symptoms of mental disorders in adults, such as extreme shyness, nervousness, strange eating habits, repetitive behaviors, and temper outbursts, can occur as a normal part of a child's development. As I said earlier, children are not simply little adults. When making a psychological diagnosis, it is important not to impose adult behavioral and emotional standards on children.

A third factor that makes diagnosis difficult is that children develop and mature at significantly different rates. "Normal" is a big tent when it comes to cognitive, emotional, and behavioral development. For children with developmental delays, interventions such as speech therapy, social skills classes, behavioral therapy, or tutoring are likely more appropriate and effective than medication.

PREVALENCE OF MENTAL DISORDERS IN CHILDREN AND ADOLESCENTS

Approximately 20 percent of children (3-17 years old) living in the United States experience a mental disorder in a given year. Put another way, that means that one out of every five children in the United States meets criteria for a major mental illness.[2] Fifty percent of all lifetime mental disorders begin by the age of fourteen, while 75 percent begin by the age of twenty-four.[3] Attention deficit hyperactivity disorder is the most prevalent condition in children while anxiety disorders are the most prevalent among teens. Suicide, of which mental illness is a major precipitating factor, was the second leading cause of death among adolescents aged fifteen to nineteen years old in 2014.[4] While mental illness is a significant public health issue that negatively impacts the lives of over seventeen million children and youth, it is estimated that only 20 percent of these individuals ever receive the treatment they need.[5]

WHAT CAUSES A MENTAL DISORDER?

Mental disorders result from a complex interaction of biological (nature) and environmental (nurture) factors. All children are born with differing degrees of biological vulnerabilities or predispositions for developing mental-health difficulties and disorders. Some individuals have a greater set of biological vulnerabilities than others. Having a biological predisposition for developing a mental disorder is not enough by itself to produce the illness. Instead, an individual's biological vulnerability must interact with environmental triggers (e.g., trauma) in order to prompt the onset of the illness. The greater the underlying biological vulnerability a child is born with, the less environmental stress is needed to trigger the onset of the illness. Conversely, in children born with a smaller biological predisposition, greater environmental influence is required to produce the disorder. Until they reach this critical level of life stress, people generally function normally, and their biological vulnerability will remain hidden.

CURE VERSUS RECOVERY

Mental disorders are chronic conditions, meaning that while we are presently able to treat or manage the afflicted individual's symptoms, we are unable to cure them. For other chronic conditions such as Type 1 diabetes, asthma, and hypertension, treatment is equivalent to symptom management. The same is true for mental disorders. The good news, however, is that a majority of individuals with mental illness (60-80 percent) who receive treatment do report some level of symptom reduction.[6] But I imagine that parents and their children are looking for more than simply symptom management—they are seeking recovery.

The Substance Abuse and Mental Health Services Administration (SAMHSA) defines recovery as "a process of change through which individuals improve their health and wellness, live a self-directed life, and strive to reach their full potential."[7] The goal of recovery goes far beyond symptom reduction but aims at equipping the child to live beyond their illness. The most important thing to remember is that recovery is a process. It takes time, can be messy, and differs from child to child, but children with mental illness can and do recover.

Figure 2.1 is a simple diagram I use with families to explain the mental-health recovery process. While this process is common, each child and family's recovery experience is unique and may differ. The top line is the process for the child or adolescent struggling with mental illness. The bottom line shows how the family's relationship with their child is affected by the stage of their recovery.

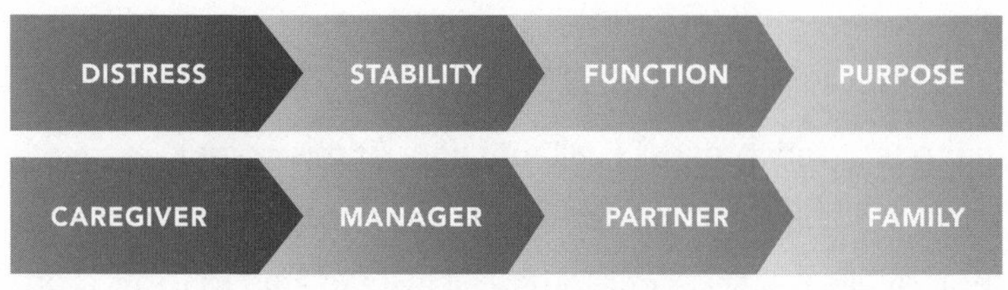

Figure 2.1. The mental health recovery process

Let's look at the top line first. At the far left side of the process is *distress*. When a child or adolescent is in psychological distress, they are experiencing unpleasant feelings or emotions that significantly affect their normal level of functioning. In other words, the child is unable to cope with the stressors and demands of daily life. At the extreme height of psychological distress, a child may have suicidal thoughts and require hospitalization. Distress is the beginning of the recovery process. Family members at this point in the process are reduced to little more than *caregivers* tending to their child's most basic needs (e.g., food, safety, shelter).

As the afflicted child begins to receive treatment, their symptoms are lessened, and they become stable. *Stability* is defined as a decrease in unpleasant feelings and emotions with an associated improvement in daily functioning. To achieve this change, the child or adolescent is cooperative with some level of treatment. At this point in the recovery process, the family's relationship has changed from one of caregiver to *manager*, meaning they are managing their child's treatment. Without the family's support (management), the child's improvement would not continue, and they would deteriorate back into distress.

As the child continues to improve, they move to the stage in the recovery process I call *function*. At this point in recovery, both the child and his family are less concerned about pathology, illness, and symptoms, but instead start to focus more on personal strengths and wellness. The family's relationship with their child is now that of a *partner* in their recovery. No longer is the child fully dependent on another for care but is empowered to get better through the support of others.

At the last stage in the recovery process, we find *purpose*. Here the child has rediscovered a sense of personal identity separate from their disorder. The child is participating in the local community (e.g., school) at a normal level and is striving to build a meaningful and satisfying life. At this point, the family has regained their *familial* relationship with the child. In other words, Mom can be Mom again, not a caregiver or manager.

This process takes time and is messy. It is never a steady progression from one stage to the next. There will be set backs and challenging periods, but recovery is possible. Understanding where you are in the process, as well as what the family relationship is at any given point, helps define more realistic expectations for you and the child.

DEVELOPING A HOLISTIC MENTAL-HEALTH RECOVERY PLAN

Children are created as the union of a physical body with an immaterial mind and spirit. Because of this, they require a holistic approach to care that takes into account all aspects of their being: physical, mental, spiritual, and relational.

The first step in developing a holistic mental-health recovery plan is to create a routine: meals, medications, school, exercise, sleep (wake-bedtime), activities/hobbies, spiritual growth, and community (social interactions). Daily structure and routine help children thrive. Because of attentional and memory problems (due to their disorder or medication), some children and adolescents may need to physically see a schedule of things they are going to do that day to be successful. The physical, mental, spiritual, and relational needs listed are issues and problems common to all mental-health problems.

Physical. Help the child be disciplined in taking their medication, getting plenty of sleep, eating healthily, and being physically active. Keeping the body (and brain) healthy will help take the edge off symptoms related to the disorder and can enhance the action of psychiatric medication.

Mental. A structured approach to psychological needs is just as important as physical needs and includes regular psychosocial treatment, enjoyable activities (e.g., art, music, writing, garden work, other hobbies, etc.), and opportunities for humor and joy.

Spiritual. Spiritual encouragement should focus on who they are in Christ (identity) and the hope that they have in him, not what they must do for God. It's time for them to be loved by God—not fight their illness (which they cannot cure on their own). Look past their disorder; encourage them and their faith.

Relational. Comfort, encouragement, and support are vitally important in recovery for both parents and child. Actively seek supportive individuals or a faith community that can encourage and care for the family.

PSYCHIATRIC MEDICATION IN CHILDREN

God created a part of us biological, and he can choose to remedy our problems through biological treatments. Taking medication, when necessary, is simply making wise use of the abundant resources provided to us by a loving Father. Mental illnesses are brain disorders and chemical imbalances that often require medication for recovery. Unfortunately, psychiatric medications only treat the symptoms of mental disorders; they do not cure the underlying neurobiological problem.

Minimizing the symptoms of the disorder, however, allows the child or adolescent to function more normally. Every person responds differently to medications, and it is normal to try several different medications until we find the ones that work best for the child. While researchers are trying to clarify how early treatment affects the developing brain, parents and doctors should weigh the benefits and risks of using medication.

For a medication to be approved by the Food and Drug Administration (FDA), the drug's manufacturer must provide the agency with clinical data demonstrating that the drug is both safe and effective in treating a specific problem in a particular group of individuals. Based on this information, the drug's label lists proper dosage, potential side effects, and approved ages for use. Unfortunately, the majority of psychiatric medications have not been approved by the FDA for use in children. However, doctors may prescribe medications as they feel appropriate, even if those uses are not included on the drug's label. This is called off-label use. Research shows that the off-label use of psychiatric medications can be helpful in many children.[8]

SATAN AND THE DEMONIC

If you are a person of faith, you are likely also concerned about the spiritual diagnosis of childhood mental illness as well. You may have thought or perhaps others have suggested to you that a child's mental disorder is the result of some spiritual weakness or demonic attack. Much like modern-day believers, the people of biblical times struggled with understanding the spiritual aspects of mental illness.

The ancient Hebrews knew that God had promised madness as one of the possible divine punishments for not obeying his commands (Deuteronomy 28:28; Zechariah 12:4), but they struggled with differentiating madness as a result of divine punishment and madness as a result of natural causes.

So individuals deemed mad or insane were generally seen as unrighteous and suffering under divine punishment. By Jesus' time, insanity was still thought to be primarily spiritual in nature but was more closely associated with the work of demons than divine punishment. We see this illustrated in John 10:20, where Jesus himself is accused of having a demon and being insane. The clear implication here is that the people of Jesus' time believed demonic possession to be at least one, and likely the primary, cause of insanity. The Scriptures, however, differentiate between natural illness and demonically caused infirmity (Matthew 8:16; Mark 1:32-34), although the Gospel writers blur the lines between the two and describe both as requiring healing (Matthew 4:24).

It is unclear from the Scriptures how to differentiate between a natural illness and one caused by demonic influence since the biblical writers often blur the line between the two. In both instances, the afflicted person is described as requiring "healing." And some relief seems possible through physical remedies, even for demonically caused illnesses. We see that music was therapeutic in Saul's case (1 Samuel 16:23), while Job found some relief by draining his boils (Job 2:8).

All mental disorders result from the interaction of biological and environmental factors. We have a biology that is broken because of sin, and we live in an environment corrupted by the evil one. From this perspective, the demonic is involved in all illness, including mental disorders, at some level, and that reality may be why the Gospel authors so blurred the lines between natural illness and demonic infirmity. The good news, however, is that Jesus has overcome the world (John 16:33) and is sovereign over Satan and the demonic (Matthew 28:18). For those who are in Christ, Satan has no direct authority. Our response as believers should be the same in all cases of illness; submit ourselves to God, pray against demonic influences, and ask God to heal the afflicted individual, be that supernaturally or through the physical remedies he has so graciously provided for us.

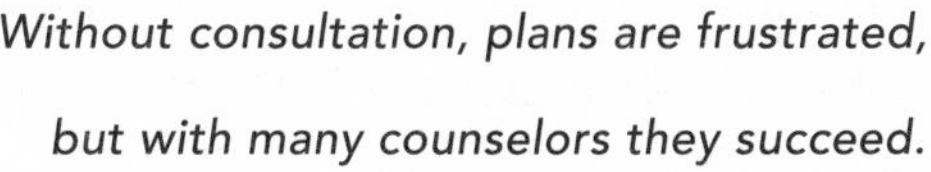

3

Questions and Answers

Without consultation, plans are frustrated,

but with many counselors they succeed.

PROVERBS 15:22

THE GOAL OF THIS CHAPTER is to provide the specific information families need to find and access effective mental-health care. The mental-health-care system is badly broken. Rather than a true continuum of care, we have a disconnected set of mental-health resources. Families often tell me they find it difficult or impossible to find care for their struggling children.

If you are a parent, my hope is that the information here is encouraging and serves as a starting point for your child's recovery. If you are a pastor or minister, these are likely the questions you are being asked by desperate parents. For you my hope is that this information enhances your ability to offer comfort and the love of Christ to weary families.

How do I know if my child's problems are serious?

Many everyday stressors can cause changes in a child's behavior. It is important to be able to tell the difference between typical emotional and behavioral changes and those associated with more serious problems. Ask yourself the following questions: Is my child's behavior impairing their ability to function in any one of the major areas of life: at home, at school, or with friends? Is my child functioning in a way that is typical for a child their age? Does my child regularly react in a way that is out of proportion in intensity to the situation that triggered the reaction? If the answer is yes to any of these questions, then seeking professional mental-health care may be warranted. Most importantly, trust your own instincts; no one knows your child better than you do.

What is the first thing I should do if I'm concerned my child may have a mental-health problem?

If there is a concern that your child is showing the symptoms of a mental-health problem, the first step in treatment is to rule out or alleviate any medical conditions that can cause, mimic, or worsen a mental disorder (e.g., infectious mononucleosis, hypothyroidism, anemia). This is done through a physical examination by a physician and appropriate laboratory tests. Once other medical conditions have been ruled out, the child should be assessed by a mental-health-care provider.

Is there a test for mental illness?

In many ways, a psychological assessment is similar to other medical tests. If a patient has physical symptoms, a physician may order X-rays or blood tests to determine the cause. Similarly, a psychological assessment is ordered to evaluate problem thinking, learning, and behavior. The assessment may include interviews, observation, pencil and paper tasks, puzzles, drawing, and games. The assessment will evaluate many skill areas, including general intellectual functioning, language, learning and memory, problem solving, planning and organization, fine motor skills, visual-spatial skills, and academic skills (reading, math, spelling, and writing). It may also include an examination of mood and behavior. The results of the assessment will inform diagnosis and the development of a treatment plan for the child.

Can my child's condition improve?

The simple answer to this question is yes. While a number of factors, including age, gender, the severity of the illness, physiological variability, and the treatment approach used influence recovery, research has clearly demonstrated that the vast majority of children and adolescents who receive treatment do show clinical improvement. In addition, children and adolescents who receive treatment recover more quickly and are less likely to relapse than those who receive no treatment. It is important to remember that recovery can be a slow process, usually months and years rather than days and weeks.[1]

Are my child's problems caused by something I did?

Parental guilt concerning fault is common following the diagnosis of a childhood mental disorder; however, your child's mental illness is not your fault. To overcome this guilt, parents often adopt attitudes toward the child's disorder that are reflective of how they believe they have failed the child. Fathers, for example, tend to see the disorder as resulting from a lack of discipline or training. They often become strict and punitive toward the child's symptoms and behaviors. In other words they want to punish the illness out of the child. Mothers on the other hand tend to view the illness as resulting from a lack of love and care. They will often ignore problem behaviors and minimize the seriousness of the child's distress. In a sense, moms want to hug it out of them. Neither of these views is accurate or helpful, both hinder recovery, and because they are in conflict with one another, they put enormous stress on the family as a whole.

Research has demonstrated that psychological disorders are the result of a complex interaction between environmental or experiential factors (such as life events) and genetic vulnerabilities.[2] No single life event (e.g., divorce) on its own is sufficient to cause mental illness, and you cannot control the genes you pass to your child. Let yourself off the hook. This is not your fault. Even perfect parenting cannot prevent mental illness. The important thing to remember is that as a parent you have a vital role to play in the recovery of your child.

What are the differences between mental-health professionals: psychiatrists, psychologists, therapists, and counselors?

Mental disorders are most effectively treated with a combination of psychiatric medication and psychosocial treatment. For that reason, a team of several mental-health-care providers with different training and specializations may be needed for your child. The following is a list of common types of providers.

Child and adolescent psychiatrist (MD or DO). A medical doctor with specialized training in the diagnosis and treatment of mental-health problems in children and teens. Psychiatrists are trained to make diagnoses and prescribe medication for the treatment of mental disorders.

Child psychologist (PhD or PsyD). A psychologist with a doctoral degree in child psychology from an accredited graduate program in clinical psychology. Psychologists are trained to make diagnoses and provide individual and group therapy. They also provide psychological and neuropsychological assessments.

Licensed clinical social worker (LCSW). A therapist with a master's degree from an accredited graduate program in social work. Clinical social workers are trained to make diagnoses, provide individual and group therapy, and provide case management and advocacy.

Licensed professional counselor (LPC). A counselor with a master's degree in psychology or counseling. Licensed professional counselors are trained to diagnose and provide individual and group counseling.

How do I find a mental-health provider for my child?

It is important that a child see a mental-health provider who is specially trained to work with children and adolescents. They should also have experience working with the child's particular mental-health problem (e.g., OCD). Talking with a child's pediatrician is a good place to start. They can often provide referrals to mental-health providers who work with children and adolescents. If the family has health insurance, their company likely has a list of mental-health-care providers in your area. Many insurance companies make the list of providers they cover available on the internet. If neither of those options work, search the online directories of mental-health providers available from professional organizations such as the American Association of Christian Counselors (aacc.net), American Psychiatric Association (psychiatry.org), or American Psychological Association (apa.org).

I don't have health insurance or the financial resources to pay for my child's mental-health care. What can I do?

A child or teen may be eligible to receive health-care coverage through Medicaid. Medicaid is an insurance program offered by the federal and state governments. It helps low-income individuals in certain groups pay for medical care and prescriptions. Low-income persons are not the only group to receive Medicaid. There are several other qualified groups that are covered, including pregnant women, women with children under six, children between the ages six to nineteen, young adults up to age twenty-one living alone, and those who are blind or deaf. Many children can receive Medicaid even if they are not otherwise eligible through a state's Children's Health Insurance Program (CHIP). For information on Medicaid or CHIP, go online to HealthCare.gov.

Free and charitable clinics are another mental-health-care option for those without insurance or financial resources. These nonprofit organizations serve as a medical safety net offering services for free or at a highly reduced cost. You can find free and charitable clinics in your area by visiting the National Association of Free and Charitable Clinics website (nafcclinics.org).

Finally, medical schools and university community psychology clinics provide another opportunity to access low-cost mental-health care. At these institutions, students and interns meet with clients at a highly reduced rate. These students are under the supervision of a licensed professional. For more information on these services, contact your local medical school department of psychiatry or university department of psychology.

How do I deal with my child's destructive behavior?

It is important to recognize that destructive behaviors in a child with a psychological disorder are the result of the disorder, not the child. These behaviors stem from biological brain abnormalities and chemical imbalances that lead to distorted thoughts, feelings, and perceptions. Destructive behaviors commonly associated with childhood psychological disorders include alcohol and substance abuse, self-harm (e.g., cutting), violence, stealing/shoplifting, and sexual promiscuity. Talk to the child's psychiatrist. Medications such as selective serotonin reuptake inhibitors (SSRIs) and mood stabilizers can be used to decrease impulsive behavior and treat associated problems such as depression and emotional instability. Monitoring a child's medication, symptoms, and side effects is essential to help minimize this type of behavior.

Appropriate boundaries must also be put into place so destructive behaviors do not harm or take advantage of you or others. Before new boundaries are implemented, a family needs to discuss and agree on the consequences for destructive and negative behavior. By setting up and consistently enforcing boundaries for a time, you are equipping the child with stability rather than allowing the disorder to control their life. The purpose of boundaries is to help a child develop a safe and healthy lifestyle, not to take away their freedom.

Keep reminding yourself this is not personal. The normal reaction is to believe that they are doing and saying destructive things to harm or disrespect you, but behind their negative words and behaviors they are actually suffering and crying out for help. Respond to the problem (the child's mental illness as a whole) rather than react to specific destructive behaviors. Avoid ultimatums and recognize that change will come as a result of a process rather than a quick fix. You don't have to be perfect—just willing to see the child through God's eyes.

What questions should I ask my child's therapist?

A therapist should make a child and family feel comfortable and at ease. A family should feel a sense of hope when working with the child's therapist. Good rapport with the therapist is extremely important. If the relationship is strained, it is not in the child's best interest. If a family feels uncomfortable with a therapist or doesn't feel like the child is benefitting from the therapist's care, they should consider switching to a different therapist. Here are a set of questions that should be asked by parents at the beginning of a child's treatment.

- What therapeutic approach do you normally use for this problem?
- Will my child be given a formal diagnosis, and will I have knowledge of that diagnosis?
- What will a typical session with you be like for my child?
- How involved will I as a parent be in the therapy?
- How will my child's progress be measured?
- How soon should I expect improvement?
- How long do children with this problem usually stay in therapy with you?
- What should I be doing at home to help support my child's treatment?
- Will you work collaboratively with my child's psychiatrist?

What questions should I ask my child's psychiatrist?

A good child and adolescent psychiatrist spends an adequate amount of time with their patients during appointments, is respectful of the family's concerns and feelings, stops medications if they haven't worked after a reasonable period of time, communicates with a child's therapist, sees a child frequently if they are in distress, and schedules appointments quickly when there is a crisis or emergency. The following are questions that parents should ask a child's psychiatrist at the beginning of treatment.

- How often will you see my child?
- Will you work collaboratively with my child's therapist?
- Will my child be given a formal diagnosis, and will I have knowledge of that diagnosis?
- Why did you select the particular medication prescribed?
- How will I know if the medicine is working or not working?
- How soon should I expect improvement?
- What are the side effects of the medication, and what should I do if they occur?
- Will side effects change as my child continues to take the medication?
- What should I do if my child misses a dose?
- How should I contact you if there is a problem?

- If there is a crisis or emergency after-hours and I cannot reach you, what hospital do you recommend we go to?

Will my child have to take medication forever?

Psychiatric medications are not a magic bullet. They only minimize problem symptoms; they do not directly treat the underlying cause of the disorder. Because children's bodies and brains are still developing, the benefits versus the risks (i.e., negative side effects) of medication must be carefully considered. The duration of pharmacotherapy varies based on the child, their circumstances, and the disorder being treated. While some disorders may require lifetime management using medication, others will need only an acute period of treatment. In either case, a family should be aggressive in pursuing other forms of care for their child, such as psychosocial treatment and lifestyle changes, to give them the best chance of discontinuing medication at some point in the future.

What about alternative treatments such as nutritional supplements?

Proper diet and nutrition are important factors in recovering from a mental disorder. A healthy diet replenishes electrolytes and amino acids. This in turns affects neurotransmitters in the brain and can help facilitate the effects of psychiatric medication. While I certainly understand a parent's concern about giving a psychoactive medication to their child that may have significant side effects, the fact is that few nutritional supplements have been shown to be effective in treating the symptoms of mental disorders. Most are unable to cross the blood-brain barrier and are simply excreted from the body unused.

Nutritional supplements are regulated by the federal government as food, not pharmaceuticals, and vary significantly in quality and composition, so unlike a medication for which you need a physician's prescription and get at the pharmacy, you cannot always be sure what you're getting at the local health-food store. That having been said, some nutritional supplements have been studied and shown to be helpful for some psychological disorders and symptoms. Three of the best are Phenibut (β-Phenyl-γ-aminobutyric Acid), 5-HTP (5-hydroxytryptophan), and omega-3 fatty acids.

Phenibut is a derivative of the naturally occurring inhibitory neurotransmitter gamma-aminobutyric acid (GABA). It was discovered in the Soviet Union in the 1960s and is still sold there as a pharmaceutical agent to treat anxiety-related disorders (e.g., panic disorder). Most GABA supplements do not cross the blood-brain barrier, but the addition of a phenyl ring to Phenibut allows it to cross from the circulatory system into the brain. Phenibut reduces anxiety, and it's only reported side effect is an increase in sleepiness. Phenibut exerts its effects by stimulating GABA receptors much like a benzodiazepine (e.g., Xanax).[3]

5-HTP is a naturally occurring amino acid and the first step in the biosynthesis of the neurotransmitter serotonin (5-HT) from tryptophan. 5-HTP is useful for the treatment of depression by causing an increase in serotonergic functioning in the central nervous system. The effect is similar to that of a selective-serotonin reuptake inhibitor. When taken with antidepressant medication, 5-HTP can cause a dangerous condition known as serotonin syndrome.[4]

The two main *omega-3 fatty acids* in fish oil, eicosapentaenoic acid (EPA) and docosahexaenoic acid (DHA) have important biological functions in the central nervous system. Omega-3 fatty acids are known to decrease the effects of systemic inflammation, and it is thought that this effect is beneficial for several mental disorders. Research has shown that omega-3 supplementation is helpful in mood disorders such as depression and bipolar disorder. Less evidence exists but several studies have also shown these fatty acids to be beneficial for ADHD and borderline personality disorder.[5]

While there is little to no evidence for the use of most nutritional supplements in mental disorders, these three do seem to be helpful. You should also always check with a child's psychiatrist before giving them any nutritional supplement.

How do I know if my child is suicidal?

If you are concerned that a child may be suicidal, talk to them! Ask specifically if they are (1) having suicidal thoughts or ideas, or (2) have a plan to do so, and (3) have access to lethal means (e.g., pills, weapons). Asking a child the "suicide question" does not increase their risk of suicide and may save their life.

If their response makes you believe they are suicidal, contact their mental-health-care provider. If they do not have a mental-health-care provider or are in immediate danger of harming themselves, take them to an emergency room or call 911. If you need to talk to someone about a child's suicidal thoughts or behavior or you need guidance on how to respond, help is only a phone call away (1-800-273-TALK).

How do I know if my child needs to be hospitalized?

Parents are naturally concerned, frightened, and confused when inpatient treatment is recommended for a child. Children or adolescents who threaten or try to take their lives, hurt themselves or others, are hallucinating, are delusional (believing things that are not true), have not eaten or slept for several days, or are unable to care for themselves (e.g., getting out of bed, bathing, or dressing) may require short-term hospitalization. It is important to understand that the goal of inpatient treatment is to stabilize a child enough so that they can be discharged to outpatient care. Unfortunately, a short-term hospitalization is not going to fix a child's mental-health problems. At best, the child's symptoms or behavior will improve slightly. A short-term psychiatric hospitalization is more about safety than cure.

How do I talk to the rest of the family about my child's mental-health issues?

When you talk to a child's siblings, use words that are right for their age and that they can understand. Explain that an illness has changed the way their brother or sister acts and feels.

Be careful not to burden children with too much information, but respect their questions and concerns. When speaking with adult family members, mental-health issues should be treated like any other health concern a child might have. Due to stigma and misinformation so prevalent in our society, be prepared to educate them about the child's particular mental-health problem. Remember that the problem symptoms of a mental disorder are the result of a medical condition; they are not the child's identity. No one says, "I am cancer"; they say, "I have cancer." No matter the issues or symptoms a child is struggling with, you can confidently say, "My child is not a disorder; he has a disorder." Children are not defined by the disorder that afflicts them. Mental-health difficulties do not hold God back from working in a child's life. Wrongly held views and beliefs (stigma) are hurtful. Don't own them.

In some cases, siblings or other family members may be asked to take part in the child's treatment. If the treatment is home-based or involves new skills in the home, it will be helpful if the family understands and supports the child. However, it is vital to help a child feel safe and to protect their privacy even within the family setting.

Where can I find support for myself?

Caring for a child with mental-health difficulties takes a significant amount of time and energy. It is common for parents to feel physically tired, emotionally spent, and spiritually empty. Parents and caregivers often say that talking to other parents dealing with the same issues is the most useful form of support. A support group is a safe place where people with common experiences or concerns provide each other with encouragement, comfort, and advice. The benefits of a support group were never more clearly demonstrated to me than in the experience of Jean and her son Thomas.

Jean, a single, middle-aged woman began attending a weekly caregiver support group that I was facilitating. Her son Thomas had been diagnosed with schizophrenia when he was twenty-two. Now twenty-eight years old, he lacked insight into his disorder and did not believe himself to be ill. The stress of the illness had been too much for Jean's struggling marriage, and she divorced four years earlier. Thomas's paranoid delusions had also driven his family and friends away. Jean was all he had left, and she was barely holding it together. She had heard about the group through her church and cautiously came that Monday night. She attended two or three times before she shared, but when she did, the story was heartbreaking. One week earlier Thomas had left the house and never returned. He took nothing with him and left his phone in his room. She said, "I honestly don't know if he is alive or dead." Every week for the next three months the group received the same report from Jean, no news on Thomas. Over those three months I saw the group rally around a woman they barely knew. They comforted and encouraged her. They prayed with and for her. They called her during the week and invited her out to lunch. These hurting caregivers were truly the physical hands and feet of Jesus to Jean in a very dark time. You could see the effect on her each week. Rather than arrive hopeless, overwhelmed by fear for her son, she was content that God was present in the situation. She was even able to minister to others in the group as they shared their problems and concerns. One Thursday afternoon, three months after he left, Thomas called Jean from San Diego (1,500 miles away) and asked her to send him money for a bus ticket to come home. We all rejoiced that following week! Support groups are a great opportunity for us to answer Christ's call to "bear one another's burdens" (Galatians 6:2).

A number of mental-health organizations offer support groups for parents and caregivers, including the National Alliance on Mental Illness (nami.org), Depression and Bipolar Support Alliance (dbsalliance.org), Grace Alliance (mentalhealthgracealliance.org), and Fresh Hope (freshhope.us). At times, a parent may need to see a mental-health-care provider themselves to receive professional counseling and support. Therapy is not weakness or failure but rather an opportunity to get healthy and recharge so that parents might better care for their child and self.

Caring for a child with a mental disorder requires that we draw deeply from God's unconditional love and unlimited grace. While we may casually throw these terms around in our church circles, they are life-giving mysteries that provide hope in the darkest of days. Our faithful Father meets us in our deepest suffering. We are never hidden from him, never too far away to be fully and completely loved. From Genesis to Revelation, God reveals the depth of his love for each of us. John 3:16 clearly states, "God so loved the world, that He sent His only begotten Son," Jesus. God does not cast aside or forget those he loves. His love is generously lavished on us even when he knows we will disappoint him. That is grace! Like Jean experienced, God's love can sustain us in the darkest of hours, the most difficult of circumstances. We are never outside his unlimited grace because grace cannot be earned, only received. Our circumstances may be a mess, unsettling, even heartbreaking, but circumstances do not have the final word. Christ, who is in us, has the final word, and his word for us is *hope*! He redeems ashes for beauty. Even death does not have the final word because Christ holds us for eternity when our life is hidden in his.

It is likely that you have many more questions. Search for the answers! Some good sources of information are your psychiatrist, pharmacist, WebMD, drug company websites, and mentalhealthgateway.org. Keep asking questions, and never give up on your child.

Above all else, surrender your situation to the Lord; "Come to Me, all you who are weary and heavy-laden, and I will give you rest. Take My yoke upon you and learn from Me, for I am gentle and humble in heart, and YOU WILL FIND REST FOR YOUR SOULS. For My yoke is easy and My burden is light" (Matthew 11:28-30). Lay your burden at the cross and ask Christ to open and close doors of doctors, therapists, psychologists, teachers, psychiatrists, and friends as you journey with your child. You are not alone. You are known by the King of the universe. He loves you and knows your child's name.

4

Different

Autism Spectrum Disorder

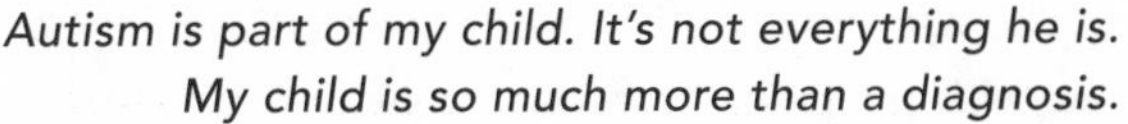

Autism is part of my child. It's not everything he is.
My child is so much more than a diagnosis.

S. L. COELHO

THIS WASN'T HOW Linda, the daughter of a pastor, had dreamed her adult life would begin: single, pregnant, and abandoned by her drug-using, abusive boyfriend. Every Sunday, nineteen-year-old Linda felt the sting of the shaming glances from those in her church. Living with her parents, her pregnancy was normal, as was the cesarean delivery. Her son, Stephen, had a normal Apgar score at birth and, with the exception of crossed eyes, appeared normal and healthy. At nine months, he received surgery to correct his eyes. Before Stephen turned one, Linda moved in with her college-age cousin and began the life of a single, working mom.

All of Stephen's developmental milestones were delayed. He crawled late, walked late, and talked late. Linda said that Stephen's pediatrician didn't seem concerned about the developmental delays, and since she had never been around small children, she didn't really know what to expect. By age five, Stephen was an active and talkative little boy ready for kindergarten.

The rigid structure and educational expectations of school quickly revealed Stephen's problems. He wasn't able to keep up with his peers academically, and he began to act out aggressively, at one point striking another student in the class. Linda was called into a meeting with Stephen's teacher and the school counselor. The school counselor labeled Stephen as "mentally retarded" and moved him to a special education classroom.[1] They also suggested Linda take Stephen to a child psychiatrist for his temper outbursts. The psychiatrist diagnosed five-year-old Stephen with ADHD and prescribed medication. He said nothing about mental retardation. The medication had little effect. Stephen's temper outbursts got worse and began to happen at home as well. The school asked Linda to sign papers allowing them to physically restrain or isolate Stephen when he had an outburst. Linda told me she hated attending Stephen's Admission, Review, and Dismissal (ARD) committee meetings at the school. "Hearing them call him mentally retarded made me sick to my stomach."

Linda stopped Stephen's ADHD medicine in the third grade. She said she didn't feel it was working, and it was expensive. When Stephen was in the fourth grade, Linda married. The marriage lasted only four years, but it did give twelve-year-old Stephen a little brother. Linda's husband was good with Stephen, as was his family. Even since the divorce, he and his family have continued to support and care for Stephen.

The summer before the sixth grade, everything changed for the family when they moved to a new home and school district. The new school's counselor did a complete assessment of Stephen and diagnosed him with autism spectrum disorder. This was the first time Linda had heard the term *autism* in relation to Stephen. Stephen was placed in a special education class and a detailed behavioral therapy plan was developed for him. Linda said the way the two different schools viewed Stephen was like night and day. Stephen was still having temper outbursts and significant problems with anxiety, but now there seemed to be hope for a better future.

CHARACTERISTIC SYMPTOMS

Autism Spectrum Disorder (ASD) is characterized by marked difficulties in social interaction and communication, and a tendency to engage in restricted, repetitive patterns of behavior. Because autism is viewed as a spectrum or continuum, deficits in these two core areas vary from mild to severe among children and adolescents.

Social interaction and communication. Problems with social interaction and communication are the most common sign of ASD. Children with ASD do not respond well to nonverbal forms of communication such as facial expressions, physical gestures, and eye contact. In addition, they have difficulty understanding that other people have different thoughts, feelings, and perspectives than they do. This makes establishing and maintaining deep relationships difficult if not impossible. Approximately 40 percent of children with ASD do not talk.[2] Those who do speak will often use language in very limited or unusual ways. They may speak only single words or repeat the same phrase over and over. Some may go through a phase where they repeat or echo exactly what they hear others say.[3] When children and adolescents with ASD do speak, they usually only talk about topics that are of interest to them, making the give-and-take of conversation difficult. Stephen, for example, is quiet most of the time, but when he does choose to speak, the content of the conversation usually has to do with video games or the military, the two topics he finds most interesting.

Repetitive behaviors. Unusual repetitive behaviors or a tendency to engage in a restricted range of activities are other characteristic symptoms of ASD. Common repetitive behaviors include hand-flapping, rocking, jumping and twirling, and arranging and rearranging objects. For children with ASD, rigidly sticking to routines and spending time performing repetitive behaviors help them to reduce uncertainty and maintain the predictability of their environment. The repetitive behaviors of high-functioning youth with ASD are often more cognitive in nature and manifest as rituals, insistence on sameness, and narrow and intense personal interests. Stephen's repetitive behaviors tend to be related to exactness and routine. For him, change is the enemy, and the routine for each day must be the same and followed without the slightest deviation or change.

DIAGNOSIS

The term *autism* was first used by Swiss psychiatrist Eugen Bleuler in 1911 to describe the withdrawal and self-absorption he observed in some individuals with schizophrenia.[4] The term was redefined in 1943 by American child psychiatrist Leo Kanner in a study of eleven children who displayed "a powerful desire for aloneness" and "an obsessive insistence on persistent sameness." Kanner referred to this condition as "early infantile autism."[5]

The diagnostic conceptualization and criteria for autism have changed dramatically over the last century. The first two editions of the *Diagnostic and Statistical Manual of Mental Disorders* (DSM-I, 1952; DSM-II, 1968) followed Bleuler's thinking and included these children under the diagnostic umbrella of schizophrenia. Kanner's work became diagnostically meaningful with the publication of DSM-III (1980), which included a new disorder, *infantile autism*. This addition gave child psychiatrists and psychologists the ability to easily differentiate autism from schizophrenia. The publication of DSM-IIIR (1987) replaced the term *infantile autism* with *autistic disorder* and provided a more expansive description of the condition. The fourth edition of the DSM (DSM-IV, 1994) included *pervasive developmental disorder not otherwise specified* (PDD-NOS) and *Asperger's disorder* along with *autistic disorder* to better represent the wide range of functioning seen in these children. The latest edition of the DSM (DSM-5, 2013) folds all previous subcategories of the condition into one umbrella diagnosis of *autism spectrum disorder* (ASD).[6] Autism spectrum disorder is classified as a neurodevelopmental disorder.[7] Neurodevelopmental disorders are a group of conditions in which the development of the central nervous system is disrupted. These disorders bridge the gap between psychiatric and neurological conditions.[8] To meet criteria for a diagnosis of ASD a child or adolescent must show (1) persistent deficits in social communication and social interaction and (2) restricted and repetitive patterns of behavior.

Stephen clearly met the criteria for ASD at a young age, but the school's counselor labeled him as "mentally retarded" or what we call today intellectually disabled. I use the term *labeled* rather than *diagnosed* because no formal assessment was done at that time, making an accurate diagnosis impossible. Stephen's strengths and potential for success were completely ignored. In the eyes of his first school, Stephen was a lost cause, a behavioral problem that needed to be controlled rather than a child with a neurodevelopmental disorder that required a specialized intervention. Many children with ASD are diagnosed through their school system, as

Stephen was, and not by a mental-health professional in the community. Regardless of who makes the diagnosis, it is imperative that parents make sure that it is based on a comprehensive behavioral and psychological assessment. Once an accurate diagnosis of ASD is given, parents must educate themselves about their child's legal rights and the special education services they are entitled to. Talking to other parents of children with autism is a great place to start.

PREVALENCE AND AGE OF ONSET

Autism spectrum disorder is estimated to occur among slightly more than 1 percent of children in the United States (1 in every 68 children). This is in line with estimates from other industrialized countries.[9] Research shows that the parents of children diagnosed with ASD typically notice developmental problems in their child prior to his or her first birthday. Even though ASD can be diagnosed as early as two years, most children are not diagnosed until after the age of four.[10] ASD is about four times more common in boys (1 in 42) than in girls (1 in 189).

The prevalence of autism in the United States has risen dramatically over the last decade. The Centers for Disease Control and Prevention's (CDC) estimate of 1 in every 68 children is more than double the 1 in 150 rate of 2000. This increase in the prevalence of ASD appears to be a global phenomenon.[11] It is likely that a large portion of this increase results from a broader definition of ASD and more effective approaches to diagnosis. Many children diagnosed with ASD today may have been misdiagnosed in the past with other conditions such as intellectual disability. As diagnoses of ASD have risen, diagnoses of intellectual disability have decreased. However, a true increase in the number of children with ASD cannot be ruled out.[12] The increase in ASD diagnosis is likely due to a combination of these factors.[13]

CO-OCCURRING CONDITIONS

Children diagnosed with ASD often struggle with additional developmental, psychological, or medical diagnoses or conditions. These conditions are sometimes described as comorbidities or comorbid disorders. The more common comorbidities associated with ASD include epilepsy, intellectual disability, gastrointestinal disorders, and mental-health problems.

Epilepsy. A *seizure* is as an abnormal discharging of the brain's nerve cells resulting in a temporary disturbance of motor, sensory, or mental function. *Epilepsy* is a condition in which a person has recurrent unprovoked seizures. Epilepsy occurs in about 30 percent of children with a diagnosis of ASD.[14] The occurrence of seizures can both precede and follow a diagnosis of ASD. Several studies suggest there are two peaks of epilepsy onset in ASD, one in childhood (< 13 years old) and a second in adolescence.[15] Intellectual disability appears to be the best clinical predictor of seizure disorder in children with ASD. The rate of epilepsy is three times greater in children who have both ASD and intellectual disability compared to children with only an ASD diagnosis.[16]

Intellectual disability. Intellectual disability is characterized by significant limitations both in intellectual functioning (reasoning, learning, problem solving) and adaptive behavior (self-care, communication, social skills). Intelligence quotient (IQ) tests are commonly used to diagnose intellectual disability. The general rule of thumb is that IQ scores ≤ 70 indicate intellectual disability. The CDC reports that 30 percent of children with ASD also meet criteria for intellectual disability.[17] While Stephen has a low IQ, he does not meet the criteria for intellectual disability.

Gastrointestinal problems. Many parents report gastrointestinal (GI) problems in their children with ASD. These problems range from chronic constipation or diarrhea to irritable and inflammatory bowel conditions. For example, children with ASD are 3.5 times more likely to suffer chronic diarrhea or constipation than are their normally developing peers.[18] Pain caused by GI problems is often recognized because of a change in the child's behavior such as an increase in self-soothing behaviors, outbursts of aggression, or self-injury. For this reason, treatments that relieve GI symptoms may be useful in reducing problem behaviors.[19]

Mental-health problems. As a group, children with ASD have a significantly higher rate of psychological disorders than that of the general population. Research suggests that approximately 70 percent of children with ASD have at least one comorbid mental disorder with as many as 40 percent having two or more comorbid mental disorders.[20] The most common comorbid mental disorders in ASD include anxiety, obsessive-compulsive disorder, and attention deficit hyperactivity disorder. Stephen struggles with comorbid ADHD, which causes him to be rather impulsive and easily distracted. Early identification of these mental-health comorbidities can aide in the development of successful targeted treatments.

RISK FACTORS

A number of risk factors have been found to increase the likelihood that a child will be diagnosed with ASD. Prenatal risk factors include obstetric complications, fetal exposure to valproic acid, and maternal metabolic conditions such as obesity, hypertension, or diabetes.[21] Research suggests that maternal metabolic conditions cause inflammation in the developing fetal brain, resulting in adverse neurodevelopmental outcomes such as ASD. Perinatal risk factors include problems during labor and delivery, extreme prematurity, and low birth weight. These are all situations or circumstances in which there is a high potential for damage to the newborn's brain. Genetic risk factors include advanced parental age at birth and genetic or chromosomal conditions such as Rett syndrome, fragile X syndrome, or tuberous sclerosis.[22] The sperm and egg cells of older parents are thought to have accumulated many spontaneous genetic mutations over time, which are passed along to the child, increasing their risk for ASD.

NEUROBIOLOGY

Heritability. Twins are often used to assess the heritability of a disorder. In twin studies the rates of a disorder in identical and fraternal twins are examined. Identical twins develop from the same fertilized egg (monozygotic), so they are genetically identical, whereas fraternal twins develop from two different eggs (dizygotic) and therefore are fertilized by different sperm. Subsequently, fraternal twins are like any traditional set of siblings and share only 50 percent of the same genes. The heritability of a disorder can be determined by looking at affected twins and determining the rate that the other twin is also affected. If there is a higher rate of concordance in identical twins compared to fraternal twins, then we can infer that genes play a role in the disorder.

Twin studies have consistently found a higher concordance rate for ASD in identical twins (approximately 90 percent of twin pairs both have ASD) when compared to fraternal twins (approximately 30 percent share the disorder).[23] Several studies have also shown that the risk of developing ASD in family members increases with the degree of biological relatedness to an affected individual. Greater risks are associated with higher levels of shared genes.[24]

Neuroanatomy. MRI studies have consistently found increased brain size in younger children with autism, followed by an abnormal growth pattern through adolescence. Children with ASD show significantly larger total brain volume prior to the age of four. This larger brain size results from increases in both gray and white matter. Whether this increased brain volume persists after age five is unclear. Several studies, however, have reported increased gray matter volume in adolescents and adults with ASD.[25] In addition, significant cortical anomalies, such as increased cortical thickness, high neuronal density, and abnormalities in cortical shape, have been observed in children with ASD.[26]

Neurochemistry. Research has shown that a number of neurotransmitters, including serotonin, dopamine, and glutamate contribute to the pathology of autism. The most consistent abnormal neurotransmitter finding in ASD involves serotonin (5-HT).[27] During early childhood, the normally developing brain appears to undergo a period of high 5-HT synthesis. This process appears to be disrupted in children with ASD who show low levels of serotonin synthesis.[28] Studies suggest that this disruption in 5-HT synthesis may lead to the miswiring of developing neural circuits involved in social cognition. Several studies have also shown altered dopamine (DA) functioning in the frontal cortex of children and adults with ASD. This dysfunction in the dopamine (DA) system may contribute to the cognitive impairment seen in ASD.[29] Research also indicates there are excessive levels of the excitatory neurotransmitter glutamate in the brains of individuals with ASD. Extremely high levels of glutamate cause the brain's cells to fire excessively.[30]

TREATMENT

While there is currently no cure for ASD, there are effective therapeutic approaches useful in managing many of the problem behaviors associated with the disorder. Early intervention can significantly lessen disruptive behaviors and equip the child with the self-help skills necessary for greater independence.

Applied behavior analysis. Applied behavior analysis (ABA) is the applied use of behavioral principles to everyday situations with the goal of either increasing or decreasing targeted behaviors. How this translates into practical application depends on the specific situation. While there are different types of ABA therapy used in treating autism (e.g., discrete trail training, early intensive behavioral intervention, pivotal response training, and verbal behavior intervention), they all share a common set of core features. These include (1) treatment beginning as early as age two, (2) intensive (20-40 hours weekly) and individualized intervention, (3) multiple behavior analytic procedures, (4) treatment delivered in a one-on-one format, and (5) parents being trained and becoming active cotherapists. Research suggests that long-term, comprehensive ABA intervention is beneficial to the intellectual, verbal, and social functioning of children with ASD.[31] Once Stephen was accurately diagnosed with ASD, a detailed behavioral therapy plan was developed for him by the school counselor. Behavioral therapy significantly improved the quality of his life and laid the foundation for his future success.

Pharmacotherapy. Although there is no medication that treats the core symptoms of ASD, a number of medications are prescribed to manage associated behavioral and emotional symptoms. Commonly prescribed medications include atypical antipsychotics (e.g., Risperdal) to reduce irritability and hyperactivity, psychostimulants (e.g., Adderall) to treat the symptoms of ADHD, selective serotonin reuptake inhibitors (e.g., Zoloft) to elevate mood and control obsessional behavior, and antiepileptic drugs (e.g., Depakote) to stabilize mood and control aggressive outbursts. Medications used in the treatment of ASD are most effective when used in conjunction with behavioral therapies. For Stephen, psychostimulants were not effective in managing the symptoms of his ADHD.

Related services. These therapies address problem symptoms commonly associated with ASD but are not specific to the disorder. They include educational therapy, speech-language therapy, sensory integration therapy, occupational therapy, physical therapy, and social-skills training. Children with ASD may benefit from a number of these therapies depending on the specific set of symptoms they display. Structured enjoyable activities may also serve a therapeutic role in children diagnosed with ASD.

During intermediate school, Stephen was allowed to participate in the Leadership Development Corps (LDC) program for a physical education credit. He loved it! LDC is a cadet-led system that follows a military structure under the supervision of an instructor. The combination of behavioral therapy and the LDC's military-style format had a significant positive effect on Stephen's behavior. Linda said his temper outbursts became few and far between. In the eighth grade, Stephen was introduced to the Special Olympics. Stephen enjoyed the competition and the opportunity to be part of a team. Stephen continued to participate in junior ROTC (Reserve Officer Training Corps) and Special Olympics throughout his high school years.

A BIBLICAL PERSPECTIVE

People of faith often look to the Bible during difficult times for guidance and comfort. The believing parents of children and adolescents struggling with mental-health problems are no different. On the pages of Scripture grieving parents find detailed accounts of a God who is present and active in the lives of children and adolescents suffering in similar ways as their own child. The goal of these biblical-perspective sections is to point you to these life-giving stories. For example, a well-known biblical story in which Jesus heals a boy with seizures offers comfort and encouragement to families caring for a disabled child.

The morning after his transfiguration on Mount Hermon, Jesus along with Peter, James, and John descended the mountain to rejoin the other nine disciples in Caesarea Philippi. When they arrived, they found a large crowd surrounding the other disciples, who were arguing with a group of scribes. Jesus asked those involved what the discussion was about. A man then called out from the crowd as he quickly moved toward Jesus. Falling at his feet, the man explained that he had brought his disabled son to the disciples and asked them to cast out the evil spirit that was causing his affliction. The disciples had failed in their attempts to heal the boy, and the scribes had taken the opportunity to discredit Jesus by questioning his power and authority.

All three of the Synoptic Gospels give details related to the boy's disorder (Matthew 17:14-18; Mark 9:17-27; Luke 9:38-43). Referring to his son as "moonstruck," the desperate father described that the boy regularly had seizures that knocked him to the ground where he would foam at the mouth, grind his teeth, and stiffen.[32] At times, he would scream and often fell into fires and water.

After rebuking the disciples and scribes for their squabbling and lack of faith, Jesus asked that the boy be brought to him. As the child approached, he suddenly was overcome by a seizure and fell to the ground. Jesus asked how long this had been occurring, and the boy's father replied, "since early childhood." Again the father begged Jesus to help his son if he was able. Jesus questioned the man's faith in his ability to heal the boy and told him that all things are possible for those who believe.

Life for the family had been difficult. The culture around them saw the boy's disorder as a curse on the family or punishment from God for sin. In the first century, seizures were thought to be contagious. It was believed they could be passed to another by simply touching or being breathed on by the afflicted person. The boy's disorder would have made the family outcasts, shunned by society. However, the love of this father for his son was greater than his circumstances. Rather than abandoning his son as a young child to regain societal honor, the father had chosen to raise him and seek a cure for his son's terrible suffering. Expensive herbal treatments and magical cures had left the family with few resources. The Jewish religious leaders had shown more contempt for the "unclean" boy than sympathy. This traveling rabbi was likely their last hope. To Jesus' statement that all things are possible to those who believe, the worn out father spoke the words that every parent of a seriously ill or disabled child has felt, "I do believe; help my unbelief." Jesus then rebuked the "deaf and mute spirit," healing the boy.

There are two lessons in relation to ASD to be learned from this biblical example. First, Jesus was moved by this suffering child. He compassionately engaged the boy's father to offer him a comforting presence. God is moved by the suffering of all children. Through his church and the Holy Spirit he offers that same comforting presence today. Second, God rewards our faith. The moonstruck boy's father had faith but was honest with Jesus about his doubts. The Scriptures tell us that faith as small as a mustard seed can move a mountain (Matthew 17:20). God is not asking for perfect faith, he is asking for "mustard seed" faith, a small faith willing to grow. Faith is the foundation on which to develop a healthy and balanced life for both parent and child.

Linda says that a positive influence on Stephen's development was a Sunday school class for children with disabilities offered at the church they attended. Stephen loved the group and formed several lasting friendships. While the special Sunday school class was beneficial to Stephen both relationally and spiritually, he was heartbroken when the church chose to stop offering the class and has refused to attend any church since. As a result, Linda has struggled to find a church for the family but says her faith has always been an anchor. Clergy have a responsibility to make sure that the faith communities they lead welcome children struggling with neurodevelopmental disorders and their families. Once in place, any modifications to or discontinuation of the groups or services offered by the church for these children must include feedback from the families before such changes are made.

THE REST OF THE STORY

Today Stephen is a happy, talkative twenty-four-year-old who lives at home with his mother and twelve-year-old brother. He aged out of high school at twenty but continues to participate in Special Olympics. While he has never been able to master reading, he does know all of his letters. He loves music, dancing, video games, and the military. Recently he began his first paying job at McDonald's. Linda said, "It's been hard, but Stephen is such a blessing." For parents of a child with ASD she said, "Education is your greatest weapon in this fight. If I had educated myself when Stephen first showed problems, those early years wouldn't have been so difficult. Also don't do this alone! Find supportive friends and family that will comfort and encourage you, build a treatment team of professionals around your child that is truly dedicated to his improvement and success, and most importantly, hold onto God."

5

Distracted

Attention-Deficit Hyperactivity Disorder

The hardest thing about ADHD is that it's invisible to outsiders. People just assume that we are not being good parents and that our child is a brat, when they don't have any idea how exhausted we truly are.

S. C.

VALARIE HAD PRAYED that her second child would be a boy. After an uneventful pregnancy and normal delivery, Mitchel entered the world. Mom, Dad, and four-year-old big sister Tamera were overjoyed with the new addition to the family. Valarie said that Mitchel was an "angel baby." She described him as "happy" and "very easy." "He rarely cried, even at night."

Around eighteen months, it became apparent that Mitchel's speech development was delayed, and he began working with a speech therapist. Valarie said that sometime between two and three years old the "angel baby" became a "tornado."

"He was full on energy all the time, constantly running around, talking excessively, impulsive, and very accident prone. He knocked his front teeth out when he was three."

Mitchel began preschool when he was three. Valarie reports that he got in trouble at school almost every day. "He simply couldn't sit still or control himself. He would wake the other kids up during naptime, he couldn't sit during circle time, and he talked constantly." The next year in prekindergarten, it was the same. Mitchel could not control his behavior. During this time Valarie first started thinking that maybe there was something wrong. This was more than "just being a boy." Other boys were able to follow the rules and be still. Why couldn't Mitchel?

Valarie met with Mitchel's kindergarten teacher before the next school year began. She explained Mitchel's history and problems with behavioral control. The kindergarten teacher worked hard that year to accommodate Mitchel's excessive energy and distractibility. He made it through the year, but it was tough. First grade was like all the other years. Mitchel got in trouble almost every day. Because he was now seven, he was starting to recognize that he was the "bad kid," and it was affecting him emotionally. Valarie decided it was time to talk to Mitchel's pediatrician.

CHARACTERISTIC SYMPTOMS

Attention-deficit hyperactivity disorder (ADHD) can be defined as a persistent pattern of inattention or hyperactivity-impulsive behavior that interferes with a child's functioning or development.[1] While all children will display some level of inattentive, hyperactive, or impulsive behavior during childhood, children with ADHD experience these behaviors more often than their same-age peers, and the behaviors are usually more serious. Prior to Mitchel beginning kindergarten Valarie had looked up ADHD on the internet and was shocked to find that her son showed virtually all the symptoms. Despite her concerns, she was hesitant to have Mitchel assessed. Looking back now, she regrets not taking action earlier.

"*Inattention* manifests behaviorally in ADHD as wandering off task, lacking persistence, having difficulty sustaining focus, and being disorganized."[2] It is not due to defiance or lack of comprehension. Inattention is often less obvious and disruptive than hyperactivity and impulsivity, so it may go overlooked for longer. Inattentive children find it difficult to process information, which distracts them from thinking and understanding. They may also find that other action around them prevents them from focusing on the task at hand.

"*Hyperactivity* refers to excessive motor activity when it is not appropriate."[3] It also includes excessive fidgeting, tapping, or talkativeness. Hyperactive children may try to do several things at once, bouncing from one activity to the next. Even when forced to sit still, which can be very difficult for them, their foot is tapping, their leg is shaking, or their fingers are drumming.

"*Impulsivity* refers to hasty actions that occur in the moment without forethought and that have high potential for harm to the individual."[4] Impulsivity may reflect a desire for immediate rewards or an inability to delay gratification. Impulsivity may manifest as social inappropriateness or as decision making with little regard for long-term consequences.

DIAGNOSIS

In a set of published lectures to the Royal College of Physicians in England in 1902, George F. Still is credited with being the first to describe the symptoms of what today we call ADHD.[5] It is important to understand that ADHD is not a new problem or disorder but has existed in medical literature for over one hundred years. One of the reasons that significant confusion and suspicion surround ADHD is that its name and diagnostic criteria have changed many times over the years.

Beginning in the late 1930s, studies of children with brain injuries resulting from a variety of causes (e.g., birth trauma, infections, lead toxicity, epilepsy, head injury) found profound cognitive and behavioral problems in these individuals. These studies ultimately led to a theory of brain injury and the term *minimal brain dysfunction* (MBD) to describe children with significant cognitive and behavioral disturbances, including the symptoms of ADHD. This designation was used until the late 1960s and publication of the second edition of the *Diagnostic and Statistical Manual of Mental Disorders* (DSM-II).

The DSM-II used a new and more specific term, *hyperkinetic reaction of childhood*, to describe a disorder that was "characterized by over activity, restlessness, distractibility, and short attention span, especially in young children." Research during the 1970s led to a better understanding of the role attention plays in the disorder, so *hyperkinetic reaction of childhood* gave way to the use of the term *attention-deficit disorder (with or without hyperactivity)* in the DSM-III. The diagnostic criteria were further refined and the name changed yet again to *attention-deficit hyperactivity disorder* with the publication of the DSM-III-R. The term *attention-deficit hyperactivity disorder* has been used to describe the disorder in all subsequent editions of the diagnostic manual (DSM-IV, DSM-IV-TR, DSM-5).

Because ADHD-like symptoms may be caused by other disorders and problems (e.g., anxiety, learning disorders, poor hearing), it is important that children displaying symptoms receive a thorough medical and psychological evaluation by a qualified professional prior to diagnosis. In the DSM-5, ADHD is broken down into three subtypes based on the predominant presenting symptom.

ADHD, predominantly inattentive presentation is characterized by six (or more) symptoms of inattention (but fewer than six symptoms of hyperactivity-impulsivity) that have persisted for at least six months. Children who are inattentive have a hard time keeping their minds on any one thing and may get bored with a task after only a few minutes. If they are doing something they really enjoy, they have no trouble paying attention. But focusing deliberate, conscious attention to organizing and completing a task or learning something new is difficult.

ADHD, predominantly hyperactive/impulsive presentation is characterized by six (or more) symptoms of hyperactivity-impulsivity (but fewer than six symptoms of inattention) that have persisted for at least six months. Hyperactive children always seem to be "on the go" or are constantly in motion. They dash around touching or playing with whatever is in sight, or talk incessantly. Sitting still at dinner or during a school lesson or story can be difficult. They squirm and fidget in their seats or roam around the room. Or they may wiggle their feet, touch everything, or noisily tap their pencil. Hyperactive teenagers or adults may feel internally restless. They often report needing to stay busy and may try to do several things at once. Impulsive children seem unable to curb their immediate reactions or think before they act. They will often blurt out inappropriate comments, display their emotions without restraint, and act without regard for the later consequences of their conduct.

ADHD, combined presentation is characterized by six (or more) symptoms of inattention and six (or more) symptoms of hyperactivity-impulsivity that have persisted for at least six months. Most children and adolescents diagnosed with ADHD have the combined type.[6]

Mitchel's pediatrician asked Valarie, her husband, and Mitchel's teacher to complete behavior rating scales to gather diagnostic information. The assessment indicated that Mitchel met criteria for ADHD (combined presentation), and the pediatrician prescribed medication. The ADHD diagnosis was like a weight lifted from Valarie's shoulders. "I finally understood him. It wasn't his fault or my fault. His brain was different. He simply didn't have the ability to control himself. I remember my mother-in-law described Mitchel's ADHD this way, 'It's like he is sitting in a room and people are throwing balls at him of varying sizes at different speeds and he is supposed to catch all of them.' That was a helpful illustration for me."

PREVALENCE AND AGE OF ONSET

Population surveys suggest that ADHD occurs in about 10 percent of children and adolescents.[7] ADHD is usually first diagnosed during the elementary school years, although children with the inattentive type are often not recognized until late childhood. Boys are twice as likely to be diagnosed with ADHD as girls.[8] While ADHD is most commonly thought of as a disorder involving children and adolescents, the symptoms can persist either fully or partially into adulthood.

RISK FACTORS

A number of environmental and psychological factors have been shown to increase a child's risk of developing ADHD. Prenatal risk factors include obstetric complications as well as maternal health problems. The children of mothers who use cigarettes or alcohol during pregnancy show a significantly higher risk for ADHD, as do children exposed to heavy metals (e.g., lead, manganese, or mercury) or organophosphate pesticides. While cigarettes contain a variety of toxic substances, nicotine is the one most associated with adverse effects on fetal development. It readily crosses the placenta and can directly affect the developing fetal central nervous system. In pregnant women who smoke, nicotine also constricts uterine arteries resulting in a decreased flow of oxygen and other nutrients across the placenta.[9]

Perinatal risk factors include problems during labor and delivery, a low Apgar score, premature birth, and low birthweight. Early life experiences such as childhood depression, a shy and withdrawn temperament, poor parent-child communication, growing up in a broken home, low socioeconomic status, parental mental illness, and acquiring traumatic brain injury all increase a child's risk of developing ADHD.[10]

It is a commonly held belief that refined sugar and food additives can cause or worsen the symptoms of ADHD, so many children with ADHD are placed on special diets and food restrictions. Studies have found that only about 5 percent of children with ADHD show improvement from dietary changes, and most of those children had preexisting food allergies.[11]

NEUROBIOLOGY

Heritability. It is well accepted that ADHD is strongly influenced by genetic factors. Twin studies have consistently found higher concordance rates for ADHD in identical twins (greater than 80 percent of twin pairs both have ADHD) when compared to fraternal twins (approximately 30-40 percent share the disorder). Research has also shown that over 25 percent of the first-degree relatives of children with ADHD meet criteria for the diagnosis themselves; this rate is only about 5 percent in the general population.[12]

Neuroanatomy. Many studies using neuropsychological techniques to look at the brain's frontal lobe functioning have discovered significant deficits in children with ADHD. These deficits include problems in attention, working memory, planning, verbal fluency, motor sequencing, and impulse control. Together these cognitive processes, controlled by the frontal region of the brain, are often referred to as "executive functions."[13] Studies using psychophysiological techniques such as electroencephalography (EEG) have found the brains of children with ADHD to be underactivated at rest and underresponsive to stimulation.[14] Similarly, brain-imaging studies of ADHD children have shown reductions in blood flow and metabolic functioning in the prefrontal regions of the brain.[15] Brain-imaging studies have also found that children with ADHD have 3-4 percent less brain volume in all brain regions, including the frontal lobes and cerebellum.[16] In summary, these studies and many others suggest that children with ADHD have problems with executive functioning as a result of abnormalities in the frontal regions of the brain.

Neurochemistry. A great deal of scientific evidence points to some type of dysfunction in the dopamine (DA) neurotransmitter system in the brains of children diagnosed with ADHD. We know that the two most common medications used to treat ADHD increase DA levels in the frontal cortex. Second, several studies have detected abnormally high levels of the dopamine transporter (DAT), a protein that regulates DA functioning, in the brains of children with ADHD.[17] A third line of evidence comes from the fact that a majority of the genes that are not functioning normally in ADHD regulate the DA system.[18] Taken together, this evidence suggests that low levels of DA functioning, particularly in the frontal brain regions, may be related to the behavioral and attentional problems seen in ADHD.

TREATMENT

There are a number of treatment options available for ADHD. In many instances, a combination of several treatments will be most effective. It's important to remember that no two children are the same, and what works for one child with ADHD might not work for another.

Behavioral therapy. The goal of behavior modification is to increase the frequency of positive behaviors and decrease the frequency of undesirable ones. This is accomplished by clearly identifying a behavior to be changed, establishing reasonable expectations (setting a goal), developing a fair system of consequences for success or failure, and applying these standards consistently. Parents, teachers, and therapists all play a role in helping the child learn how to behave appropriately. Behavior modification is a structured, intensive, and time-consuming approach to treatment. It is important to emphasize that children who receive both medication and behavioral therapy respond better to treatment, and children who receive behavioral therapy have been shown to require lower doses of medication for successful treatment compared to those who receive medication alone.

Pharmacotherapy. The most widely used medications for the treatment of ADHD are methylphenidate (e.g., Ritalin, Concerta, Metadate, Focalin) and amphetamine (e.g., Adderall, Dexedrine). These medications are classified as stimulants and have been approved by the FDA since the 1950s for treating behavioral problems in children. They appear to work by increasing activity in areas of the brain that are underactivated (e.g., frontal lobes) in children with ADHD. This increase in brain activation causes an improvement in attention and reduces impulsiveness and hyperactivity. A beneficial response is seen in greater than 70 percent of children treated for ADHD with psychostimulants. Common side effects include weight loss, decreased appetite, insomnia, headaches, and slowed growth.

While Mitchel's father was not fully supportive of him starting medication, the couple felt they had no other option. The medication the pediatrician prescribed worked. Mitchel's behavior at school improved almost immediately, but there were also negative side effects. Valarie said, "Mitchel became an emotional rollercoaster. His teachers reported that his personality changed, and he seemed 'zoned out.' He was struggling to get along with others, and by the end of the day when he came home, he was full of anger. I thought we just had to take the good with the bad." The emotional lability Mitchel experienced is a negative side effect not uncommon in children being treated with psychostimulant medications.

In the summer before Mitchel began the second grade, the pediatrician made a medication change. Mitchel was still expressing a significant amount of anger and anxiety. He was blowing up and threatening to harm others and himself. Valarie said, "He didn't know how to voice his extreme feelings." The pediatrician switched Mitchel's medication a third time and his emotions improved. Rather than intense anger, he was just "grumpy" at the end of the day.

Mitchel started meeting with a behavioral therapist during the third and fourth grade for his anger. The beginning of the fifth grade brought another change in medication. This medication, like the others, seemed to work at first, but then Mitchel became an "emotional train wreck."

During a basketball game, he started crying. "He was standing at the free-throw line weeping. He couldn't get ahold of himself. It happened at two games in a row." That was enough for Valarie. She took Mitchel to the pediatrician and stopped the medication. Valarie also met with Mitchel's teachers to let them know that he was no longer on medication and that they should expect his behavior to change. It was a rough spring semester. Mitchel's grades dropped, but not significantly. His excessive talking was a daily problem both with teachers and peers. "He wears out his friends. They get annoyed with him." According to the CHADD website,

> Children with ADHD may be rejected by peers because of hyperactive, impulsive, or aggressive behaviors. Parent training available through organizations like CHADD (Children & Adults with ADHD) can help you learn how to assist your child in making friends and learning to work cooperatively with others.[19]

A BIBLICAL PERSPECTIVE

Clinicians and historians have suggested that several individuals in the Bible, including Esau and the apostle Peter, may have struggled with the symptoms of ADHD.[20]

The son of Isaac and grandson of Abraham, Esau was born with his twin brother, Jacob, clutching his heel. An outdoorsman and hunter, Esau is also referred to as Edom in the

Scriptures due to his reddish coloring. The book of Genesis, the writings of the first-century Roman-Jewish historian Titus Flavius Josephus, and the rabbis of the Jewish Midrash all provide details related to Esau's behavior.[21]

Esau was a twin, and multiple pregnancies are fraught with risks and complications, particularly in ancient times. Both Genesis 25:22 and Josephus tell us that Rebekah, Esau's mother, had complications during pregnancy.[22] A multiple pregnancy almost never lasts the forty weeks that a single pregnancy usually takes, and over half of multiple pregnancies are delivered before thirty-five weeks. Even today the average birth weight of a twin is well below that of a single birth. So at birth Esau likely had multiple prenatal and perinatal risk factors shown to increase a child's risk of developing ADHD; obstetric complications, prematurity, and low birth weight.

The Jewish Midrash tells us that Esau and his twin were very different children. Jacob is described as a myrtle with a pleasant aroma while Esau was a wild rose with thorns. Jacob excelled in school and continued his education after the age of adulthood, while Esau struggled and ended his schooling at thirteen. And Edom (Esau) was a term used by the ancient rabbis to describe an aggressive-impulsive temperament that needed to be refined into positive action.

Perhaps the clearest example we have of Esau's problems with impulse control and inability to delay gratification is the story of the firstborn birthright. When the twins were still children, Esau returned from hunting tired and hungry to find Jacob preparing red lentil stew.[23] Esau asked for some stew, to which Jacob replied, "First sell me your birthright." Esau then said, "Behold I am about to die, so of what use is the birthright to me?" and impulsively gave away the firstborn blessing, a decision he would regret for the rest of his life. Furthermore, his impulsive personality is vividly portrayed by the text's use of four rapid-fire verbs after he receives the stew; "He ate and drank, and rose and went on his way" (Genesis 25:34). The quick succession of these four verbs in an uninterrupted sequence is a one-time occurrence never again repeated in the entire Bible. They suggest a restless child who can't sit still or remain in one place for long.

Two lessons in relation to ADHD can be learned from this biblical example. First, parental love, acceptance, and support are the foundation for a child's later success. Isaac deeply loved Esau despite his struggles (Genesis 25:28). He affirmed him for his strengths (e.g., hunting) and encouraged him in the development of those skills. His father's love would be the foundation on which Esau was able to later forgive his brother's deceit and become a leader of men. Children with ADHD often feel like the proverbial square peg in a round hole. Isaac and Esau teach us that the world needs square pegs. Focus on developing the child's strengths rather than fixing their deficits.

Second, the presence of mental-health difficulties does not alter or thwart the perfect purpose and plan God has for a child. Before his birth, God had foretold that Esau would be the leader of a great nation, and that promise was fulfilled despite his early struggles. God created each child, and he is faithful to see that the purpose and plan he ordained for their life is fulfilled. It may be difficult to see at this point, but God is in control of a child's future.

THE REST OF THE STORY

Now thirteen and in the eighth grade, Mitchel has not taken medication for three years. Valarie says, "He has been able to develop skills on his own to regulate his emotions and behavior. It is still hard though. We do three to four hours of homework a night when other kids probably complete the same assignment in an hour. It's exhausting! However, his behavior is definitely getting better as he matures. In the past six months, there has been more harmony in our family than ever before." Mitchel is also very involved in football. Recent research suggests that regular physical activity can both reduce the severity of symptoms and improve cognitive functioning for children with ADHD. "On the field he is like a different person. He is an encourager and supporter of his teammates. He is focused and successful. When he is struggling with something, I will say to him, 'Where is football, Mitchel?' and he is able to focus himself. He recognizes that on the field he is like a different person."

6

Disruptive Behavior Disorders

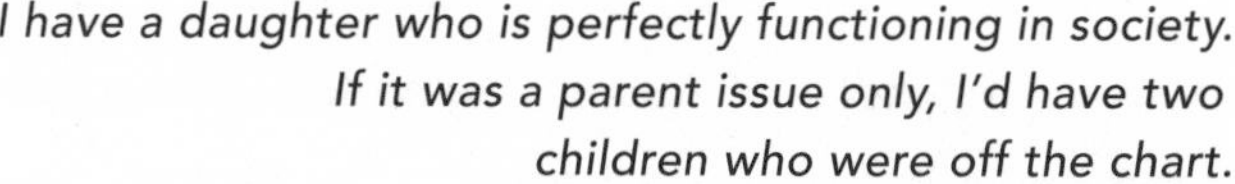

I have a daughter who is perfectly functioning in society. If it was a parent issue only, I'd have two children who were off the chart.

AMY CLULEY

DIFFICULT TIMES FOR MAX and his family began when he was in the third grade. That year his father was diagnosed with brain cancer and began treatment. Eighteen months later, years of marital conflict, infidelity, alcohol abuse, and the added stress of cancer treatment left his parents separated and ultimately divorced. At the beginning of the fourth grade, Max for the first time started getting in trouble at school. His mother, Natalia, said that he was also becoming more difficult to manage at home. Natalia scheduled a psychological assessment for Max with a local mental-health-care provider to try to find a reason for his difficult behavior. The psychologist diagnosed Max with ADHD (combined presentation) and informed his mother that he was also displaying a number of oppositional defiant symptoms. Max was placed on medication for ADHD by his pediatrician. Natalia told me that Max's behavior at school changed for the better almost immediately, although he continued to be a handful at home.

Max continued his medication during the fifth grade and had a good year. Sixth grade, as Natalia describes it, "was when the bottom dropped out." Max struggled socially at school. He was angry and irritable, and he began to take his frustrations out on his peers. As a result, the other students began to avoid him, and he became more isolated. Natalia thought his isolation was a result of the Christian school's small class size. She also thought the ADHD medicine was causing him to act out. She decided to move Max, midyear, to a public school and stop his medication. Max struggled to control his behavior, so after a meeting with his teachers, Natalia decided to put him back on the medication, and he successfully completed the year. Max started puberty during the seventh grade. Natalia says that his behavior at school was okay, but at home he was becoming increasingly angry and aggressive. Also during this year Natalia became aware Max was using marijuana.

CHARACTERISTICS SYMPTOMS

The disruptive behavior disorders (DBDs) are characterized by problems in emotional and behavioral regulation. These problems manifest as actions that violate the rights of others (e.g., aggression) or bring the child into significant conflict with societal norms or authority figures.

Emotional dysregulation. The effective regulation of emotion is necessary for mental wellness and social functioning. Every day we are confronted by individuals or circumstances that elicit emotions. Emotion regulation allows us to respond to those situations in a socially acceptable and flexible way. Children with disruptive behavior disorders are less likely to inhibit emotional reactivity and as a result use more inappropriate regulatory strategies.[1]

Defiant and hostile behavior. It is not unusual for children or adolescents to occasionally argue, be uncooperative, or even defy their parents or teachers. This often occurs when they are overwhelmed or stressed. Children with disruptive behavior disorders, however, "display a persistent pattern of defiant and hostile behavior, such as temper tantrums, fighting, cruelty, arguing, and disobedience toward parents, teachers, or other authority figures." This leads to problems at school and in relationships with others.[2]

By eighth grade, Max was smoking cigarettes and vaping as well as using marijuana, Xanax, and hydrocodone. He was kicked off the junior high golf team and suspended from school for six weeks after he was caught using the opiate-based drink "Lean."[3] At this point Max had become associated with several local drug dealers and was having Xanax and hydrocodone delivered to the house. During this same time, he had a gun placed to his head and was assaulted during a drug deal gone bad.

Unable to control Max's behavior, Natalia sent him to live with her parents, but his behavior only got worse. Although his grades were horrible, he completed the eighth grade and moved back home for the summer. Soon after, Max went off his medication, and Natalia says his behavior became "ten times worse." He added acid, cocaine, and mushrooms to his drug use, and by the end of the summer Natalia and her daughters were so scared of Max that he was sent to live with his father.

DIAGNOSIS

While descriptions of juvenile oppositional and delinquent behavior appear in our earliest historical records, the conceptualization of these problems as a mental-health issue is a more recent occurrence.[4] The basis for our modern view of the disruptive behavior disorders began with the inclusion of behavior disorders in childhood and adolescence in the DSM-II. Within this section, three disorders or reactions were described that overlap significantly with the disruptive behavior disorders: runaway reaction of childhood (or adolescence), unsocialized aggressive reaction of childhood (or adolescence), and group delinquent reaction of childhood (or adolescence). The diagnoses of oppositional defiant disorder (originally referred to as oppositional disorder) and conduct disorder were first introduced in the DSM-III. While the criteria for both disorders have changed somewhat over the years, these two disorders have been included in all subsequent editions of the DSM. In the DSM-5 the disruptive behavior disorders are described as follows.

Oppositional defiant disorder (ODD) is a pattern of angry/irritable mood, argumentative/defiant behavior, or vindictiveness exhibited during an interaction with at least one individual who is not a sibling that has lasted at least six months. This disturbance in behavior is associated with psychological distress in the child/adolescent or others in their immediate social context. The child's problem behavior may also negatively impact important areas of normal functioning (e.g., education, social).

Conduct disorder (CD) is a "persistent pattern of behavior lasting at least twelve months in which the basic rights of others or age-appropriate societal norms are violated. Disruptive behaviors associated with CD may manifest as aggression toward people or animals, destruction of property, deceitfulness or theft, or serious violations of rules. This behavioral disturbance results in a clinically significant impairment in social, academic, or occupational functioning." Children and adolescents diagnosed with CD are further classified in relation to their level of remorse or empathy. Children are specified as having "limited prosocial emotions" if they present with two or more of the following: lack of remorse or guilt, lack of empathy, lack of concern about performance in important activities, and shallow or deficient affect.[5] These children tend to show little remorse for their actions and exhibit a reduced sensitivity to punishment. Max clearly met criteria for CD by the eighth grade. Natalia says at times he seemed very remorseful for his behavior, while at other times he seemed to have no empathy for others or guilt related to his actions.

PREVALENCE AND AGE OF ONSET

The prevalence of both ODD and CD is estimated to be around 3 percent.[6] ODD appears to be slightly more prevalent in boys. The first symptoms of ODD usually appear during the preschool years. Conduct disorder is more common in boys than in girls. Conduct disorder can have its onset early, before age ten or in adolescence. Children with early onset CD (before age ten) are more likely to have behavior problems that persist into adulthood than those with adolescence onset. ODD often precedes the development of CD (this was true for Max), especially for those with the early onset type. ODD, CD, and ADHD represent the largest group of child and adolescent psychiatric referrals. Comorbidity among these disorders is common and is predictive of a poorer outcome.

RISK FACTORS

A number of psychological and environmental factors have been shown to increase a child's risk of developing ODD or CD. Prenatal risk factors include maternal smoking and alcohol use, maternal stress and anxiety, maternal illness, and obstetric complications. Perinatal risk factors include complications during labor and delivery, premature birth, and low birth weight. Childhood experiences such as exposure to violence, poverty, and stressful family events (such as the loss of a parent or divorce) have also been shown to increase a child's risk of later developing a disruptive behavior disorder.

Dysfunctional family relations, as well as parental abuse or neglect, poor parenting, parental criminality, parental substance use, and family adversity, have all been shown to increase a child's risk. Parental psychopathology (especially antisocial personality disorder and substance use) also increases a child's risk for developing ODD or CD. During adolescence, the influence of peers becomes increasingly important; disruptive behavior disorders may arise or be maintained by affiliation with deviant peers.

High emotional reactivity, difficulty controlling or regulating emotions, and problems handling frustration are also factors that have been shown to increase a child's risk. Finally, children and adolescents who are raised to believe violence is the proper means to solve problems are at an increased risk for developing ODD or CD.[7]

Max's conduct disorder followed a developmental sequence that includes many of the risk factors just mentioned. A dysfunctional family that included marital discord, alcohol abuse, and inconsistent parenting laid the foundation for the disorder. The combination of stress related to his father's cancer, ADHD, and his parent's divorce resulted in academic failure and peer rejection. These dual stressors led, in turn, to depression, involvement with a deviant peer group, and ultimately chronic delinquent behavior.

NEUROBIOLOGY

Heritability. Disruptive and antisocial behavior runs in families, suggesting that genetics may play a role. Twin studies have consistently found higher concordance rates for both ODD and CD in identical twins (greater than 60 percent of twin pairs share the disorder) when compared to fraternal twins (approximately 20-30 percent share the disorder).[8] The influence of genetic factors appears to be strongest for early onset CD.

Neuroanatomy. Brain-imaging research has found that children and adolescents with disruptive behavior disorders show abnormal frontal lobe functioning in the anterior cingulate cortex, orbitofrontal cortices, and dorsolateral prefrontal cortex. This is likely responsible for their increased risk-taking behaviors, impulsiveness, and inability to delay reward. Additionally, areas deep in the brain, especially the amygdala and insula, have been found to exhibit abnormal functioning and a smaller overall size in these children. These abnormalities likely account for the emotion dysregulation and aggressive and hostile behaviors seen in the disruptive behavior disorders.[9]

Neurochemistry. Serotonin (5-HT) is one of the brain's most important neurotransmitters for behavioral control.

Several studies have found an abnormally low level of 5-HT functioning in the brains of children and adolescents with disruptive behavior disorders. Further, these low levels of 5-HT have been shown to correlate with aggression, poor treatment outcomes, and antisocial behavior.[10] Children and adolescents with disruptive behavior disorders have also been found to have high levels of testosterone and low levels of the stress hormone cortisol (particularly in CD with high callous-unemotional traits).[11] High testosterone levels are positively related to aggression while low cortisol levels suggest that these children lack anxiety or fear.

TREATMENT

Research has shown that a combination of family and individual therapy is usually the most effective approach to treating the DBDs. When selecting a treatment, the child's age and development, severity of symptoms, any co-occurring disorder, and the child's ability to participate in treatment must be considered.

Behavioral therapy. Therapies such as parent management training and behavioral family therapy are the most well-established approaches to treating disruptive behavior disorders. In parent management training, the parents and therapist work together to develop a specific and systematic plan to change oppositional behavior in the child. Parents, family members, and other caregivers are taught techniques in positive reinforcement and ways to discipline more effectively.

These plans often include setting specific limits and boundaries, as children with ODD and CD often believe that they are entitled to behave any way they want.

Behavioral family therapy focuses on the dynamics of family members and how they contribute to family functioning and dysfunction. This therapeutic approach involves helping children and their parents understand and deal with the difficulties the child is experiencing. Children with ODD and CD often only know negative ways of interpreting and responding to real-life situations. Therapists teach children, as well as their parents, coping skills to help them manage difficult situations. Proper behavior is modeled for the children by the therapist (and later by the parents), and then children are reinforced and rewarded when they later choose to act appropriately.

Pharmacotherapy. Medication alone has not been proven effective in treating disruptive behavior disorders. However, medication may be a useful part of a comprehensive treatment plan to help control specific behaviors and to treat coexisting conditions such as ADHD, anxiety, and mood disorders. Stimulants such as methylphenidate and amphetamine are sometimes prescribed for children with ODD and CD in order to reduce impulsivity and aggressive behavior. When children and adolescents with a disruptive behavior disorder also have a mood disorder or anxiety, treatment with antidepressants and anti-anxiety medications helps lessen symptoms.

After much discussion, Max's parents decided that residential treatment was the best course of action for him. Max was sent to live at a faith-based, therapeutic community specializing in adolescent behavioral problems. After four months, his resistance to treatment and constant rule violations caused him to be kicked out of the program.

Once Max returned home, he began receiving treatment on an outpatient basis from a local psychiatrist and therapist. He was drug tested regularly, and Natalia said she never left him alone. "I even had him sleep in my bedroom so I could make sure he didn't sneak out at night." The first few weeks home from the residential program went well. Natalia said, "There was clearly a honeymoon period." Max was respectful, obedient, and compliant; after two weeks things changed for the worse. Max's behavior deteriorated. He became irritable, angry, and started using drugs again. At one point he stole his father's car and wrapped it around a telephone pole going 100 miles an hour. Several days later Natalia received a call from Max's school telling her he was acting strangely.

When she arrived, Max was "out of his mind." He was lying down in the middle of the hall and could barely walk. As Natalia was driving her son to the hospital, he jumped out of the moving car. He physically attacked his father and grandfather, who were trying to help. The police were called. Max was wild, screaming, and wetting himself. Once at the emergency room, restraints were used to hold him in the bed. It was found that Max had overdosed on a combination of

Xanax and hydrocodone. Once stabilized, Max was sent to an adolescent psychiatric facility for six days. From there he was transferred to a short-term residential adolescent substance abuse treatment program in another state. He successfully completed the fifty-nine-day program but still required additional treatment. Max was subsequently admitted to a one-year residential treatment program.

A BIBLICAL PERSPECTIVE

The Proverbs give us the Bible's best example of adolescent disruptive behavior in the description of the "foolish son." Throughout the book of Proverbs the foolish son is contrasted with the wise son. The wise son is obedient and listens to his parents' instruction (Proverbs 13:1), while the foolish son is lazy (Proverbs 10:5), disobedient (Proverbs 30:17), argumentative (Proverbs 13:1), hangs out with troublemakers (Proverbs 23:19-21; 28:7), rejects discipline (Proverbs 15:5), and mocks his parents (Proverbs 30:17). Daughters can also be foolish as we see from the deuterocanonical[12] book of Sirach 22:3: "An evil-nurtured son is the dishonor of his father that begat him and a foolish daughter is born to his loss" (KJV). Proverbs tell us that the behavior of the foolish child is not only personally harmful but also damages his family (Proverbs 10:1; 17:21, 25; 19:13).

God calls all parents to instruct and discipline their children (Proverbs 1:8; 4:1; 23:13). In most instances, this training, out of love, leads to a well-adjusted child who develops into a happy and successful adult (Proverbs 22:6). The Scriptures recognize, however, that there are instances when this child-rearing process does not go smoothly, and parents struggle to manage their child's behavior.

There are two important truths related to the disruptive behavior disorders to be learned from the description of the foolish child. First, parents need help and support when dealing with an ODD or CD diagnosis. The Bible describes the negative effects the child's behavior has on the family (Proverbs 10:1; 17:21, 25). The foolish child's parents are in despair and broken by and for their distressed child. It's tempting to judge the parents of children with disruptive behavior disorders by what they should and shouldn't do. But until you've walked a mile in their shoes, it's difficult to know the pain and shame that comes from parenting a child who simply will not obey. As the body of Christ, our focus should not be on blaming parents for their child's disruptive behavior, but rather supporting and assisting them as they intervene to save their child from a path that leads to destruction (Ecclesiastes 4:12; Galatians 6:2).

Second, there is hope! Hear the words of Proverbs 19:18, "Discipline your son while there is hope, / And do not desire his death." There is hope to change a child's behavior and alter the deadly path they have chosen. As Christians even in the midst of the storm, we can say there is hope because Christ has overcome the troubles of this world (John 16:33), and he will supply the sustaining grace you need to save a child.

Despite everything that has happened, Natalia says her faith has been strengthened: "I have learned that I am not in control." Unfortunately, their church was not supportive during this trial. "Christians do not embrace you when you have a hard kid. There was a lot of gossiping; we felt judged. Everyone saw him as the 'bad kid,' and our family was avoided. Ultimately we had to find another church."

THE REST OF THE STORY

Now sixteen years old, Max will complete the residential treatment program in the next month. Natalia speaks to Max and his therapist weekly via video conference, and he has made several weekend visits home over the last few months. On those visits Max has been respectful and obedient toward both his mother and sisters. He says that he wants a new start and seems genuine in his desire for change. Natalia is pleased with Max's progress and says she is "cautiously optimistic" about his return home. "I feel he is in a good place. I do have hope, but if I'm not careful I can quickly go to a very dark place. No matter how it turns out, I will never give up on my son!"

7

Hopeless

Depressive Disorders

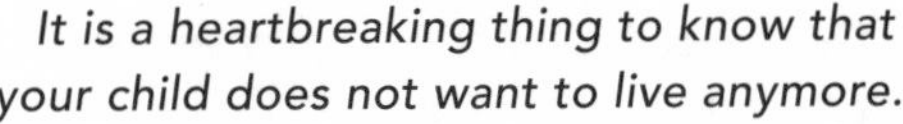

It is a heartbreaking thing to know that your child does not want to live anymore.

M. M.

ALEX BEGAN TO SHOW the first signs of depression in the eighth grade. Watching his mother suffer from a terminal illness had taken a toll on the fourteen year old. The once straight-A student was now struggling in class. He often seemed confused and unable to make decisions. He began to isolate himself at home and no longer seemed to care about things he once found enjoyable. While he had always been a picky eater, his diet now consisted of little more than a specific brand of white bread and a special type of cheese. Alex's mother passed away during the first semester of his freshman year in high school.

Richard, Alex's father, grieving the death of his wife, watched his son sink deeper and deeper into depression. "He no longer wanted to go to school. He was constantly late and received multiple detentions for being tardy." As Alex isolated himself and retreated into the world of video games, his friends began to drift way. Richard took his son to a child psychologist who diagnosed him with major depressive disorder. Soon after, Alex began weekly therapy and a child psychiatrist prescribed him an antidepressant medication. Unfortunately, he refused to take the medication.

CHARACTERISTIC SYMPTOMS

The characteristic symptom of the depressive disorders is a persistently depressed and empty mood. In children or adolescents, the mood may be irritable rather than sad. The depressive symptoms are severe enough that the child is unable to function normally.

A *major depressive episode* is characterized by either a persistent depressed mood or loss of interest or pleasure in daily activities over at least a two week period. Four or more of the following symptoms must also be present: significant weight change or change in appetite, sleeping too much or not being able to sleep, psychomotor agitation or retardation, fatigue or loss of energy, feelings of worthlessness or excessive guilt, an inability to concentrate or indecisiveness, and recurrent suicidal thoughts.

DIAGNOSIS

Prior to the 1970s, "children and adolescents were thought incapable of experiencing depression according to the dominant psychoanalytic theory. Thus depression was considered an adult disease. However, case reports from as early as the seventeenth century describe adolescents exhibiting the symptoms" of depressive disorders.[1] In 1975, a conference sponsored by the Center for Studies of Child and Family Mental Health at the National Institute of Mental Health was convened to review the literature on childhood depression. This meeting along with the pioneering work of Drs. Leon Cytryn and Donald McKnew resulted in the widespread recognition that depression is an all-too-common psychological reaction in children and adolescents.[2]

The publication of the DSM-III in 1980 first introduced the diagnostic category of mood disorders, containing distinct criteria for both the bipolar disorders and depressive disorders. In the most recent edition of the diagnostics manual (DSM-5), the depressive disorders are for the first time separated completely from the bipolar disorders and given their own category. The primary depressive disorders are major depressive disorder, persistent depressive disorder (dysthymia), and disruptive mood dysregulation disorder.

Major depressive disorder (MDD) is characterized by a major depressive episode that lasts at least two weeks, severe enough to cause marked impairment in the child's daily functioning. A person may experience a major depressive episode only once, but more commonly episodes occur several times in a lifetime.

Persistent depressive disorder (dysthymia) is a less severe form of depression that is characterized by a chronically depressed mood for at least two years. The symptoms of dysthymia, while not seriously disabling, keep the child from functioning well or feeling good. Many individuals with dysthymia experience major depressive episodes during their lives. After two years of therapy with no improvement, Alex's MDD evolved into dysthymia. He was trapped in a persistent depressive state. Alex's father, Richard, said, "The therapy didn't really make things any better, but I do believe it kept him from getting worse."

Disruptive mood dysregulation disorder (DMDD) is characterized by a chronic irritable mood and frequent, severe temper outbursts that seem grossly out of proportion to the situation. These outbursts interfere with the child's ability to function at home, in school, or with their friends. Disruptive mood dysregulation disorder was included in the DSM-5 to more accurately categorize some children who had previously been diagnosed with pediatric bipolar disorder. Children with DMDD do not experience the manic or hypomanic episodes characteristic of bipolar disorder, and they do not typically develop adult bipolar disorder later in life.

PREVALENCE AND AGE OF ONSET

The prevalence of depressive disorders in children is estimated to be 2.5 percent for major depressive disorder and 1 percent for persistent depressive disorder. Elevated risk for depression begins in the early teens and continues to rise throughout adolescence. In childhood, major depressive disorder and persistent depressive disorder occur equally in boys and girls. During adolescence, however, a gender difference is seen, with MDD and dysthymia occurring more commonly in girls than boys.[3] Disruptive mood dysregulation disorder is estimated to occur in 2 percent of children and adolescents. By definition, the onset of DMDD must be before age ten, and the diagnosis cannot be applied to children younger than six or those over eighteen. The prevalence of DMDD is higher in boys and school-age children than in girls and teens.[4]

RISK FACTORS

A number of factors have been shown to increase a child's risk of developing a depressive disorder. Prenatal and perinatal risk factors include fetal malnutrition, maternal cigarette or alcohol use, maternal stress or anxiety, maternal marijuana use, and low birth weight. Research suggests that the first trimester is a particularly sensitive period for fetal exposure to marijuana and the later development of depressive symptoms.[5] Childhood experiences such as low socioeconomic status, marital discord, emotional difficulties between one parent and the child, parental mental illness, parental loss or separation, abandonment, neglect, or physical/sexual abuse have all been shown to increase the risk for a depressive disorder.

Significant stress from negative life events, such as the death of a family member, divorce, or serious physical illness in a close relative, may play a role in triggering a depressive episode. Children and teens that have an extremely negative outlook on life marked by low self-esteem and self-defeating or distorted thinking are more likely to develop a depressive episode in response to stressful life events. This was the case with Alex. He had struggled with anxiety for many years prior to his mother's illness and death. The trauma of losing his mother overwhelmed him and triggered his depression.

NEUROBIOLOGY

Heritability. Twin studies have shown that depression becomes increasingly heritable from childhood to late adolescence. The heritability of adolescent-onset depression is similar to that seen in adult-onset. Research suggests that childhood depression is more strongly associated with environmental stressors, is less heritable, and shows a weaker association with adult depression than adolescent-onset depression. Adolescent-onset depression is strongly associated with adult depression and is best viewed as an early-onset of the adult disorder.[6] To date, no studies have assessed the heritability of disruptive mood dysregulation disorder, but several studies have looked at related issues. The results suggest that irritability, characterized by temper outbursts and negative mood, may be significantly influenced by genetic factors.[7]

Neuroanatomy. Electroencephalographic (EEG) research has found reduced left frontal electrical activity in adolescents with major depressive disorder. Decreased left frontal EEG activity reflects reduced positive emotion expression.[8] Neuroimaging studies have identified several brain structures that are dysfunctional in children and adolescents diagnosed with depressive disorders. Two of these structures, the amygdala and the subgenual anterior cingulate cortex (subgenual ACC), are part of what is called the limbic system.[9] The amygdala is involved in emotionally mediated attention, in assigning emotional significance to stimuli, and along with the hippocampus (another limbic system structure) in remembering emotionally significant events. The amygdala of children and adolescents diagnosed with depressive disorders tends to be smaller and underactive compared to normal controls.[10] The subgenual ACC influences how we experience emotions. One of its core functions is to regulate amygdala activity, preventing excessive emotional reactivity. A neural network based in the subgenual ACC that includes the frontal lobes and amygdala functions abnormally in children diagnosed with depressive disorders.

Neurochemistry. Several neurotransmitter systems have been implicated in childhood depressive disorders. Research has found that glutamate, the most common excitatory neurotransmitter in the brain, is overactive in children with depressive disorder, while gamma-aminobutyric acid (GABA), the most common inhibitory neurotransmitter in the brain, is underactive in these same individuals.[11] Studies have also shown that the serotonin system is dysfunctional in childhood depressive disorders.[12] Serotonin in the brain is thought to regulate mood and our general sense of well-being. A great deal of research in the neurochemistry of childhood depressive disorders has focused on the hypothalamic-pituitary-adrenal (HPA) axis, one of the body's major stress response systems. Studies in children and teens diagnosed with depressive disorders have consistently shown chronic HPA axis hyperactivity (e.g., higher resting cortisol levels) and an inability for this system to return to normal functioning following exposure to a stressor.[13] Together these neurochemical abnormalities result in heightened levels of anxiety and irritability, depressed mood, an inability to experience pleasure, excessive worry, and a lack of emotional control.

TREATMENT

When choosing the most appropriate treatment for a child or adolescent with a depressive disorder, the severity of depression must be taken into account. For those with mild depression, psychosocial treatment is recommended, while those with more moderate to severe depression may need therapy in combination with medication.

Psychosocial treatment. Two therapeutic approaches have been shown to be effective in treating depressive disorders in children and adolescents, interpersonal therapy (IPT) and cognitive-behavioral therapy (CBT).[14] The foundational idea of IPT is that depression can be treated by improving how a child relates to others. IPT emphasizes the way symptoms of depression are related to an individual's relationships. The goals of IPT are symptom reduction, improved interpersonal functioning, and increased social support. The goal of CBT is to help the child eliminate negative beliefs or behaviors and replace them with positive ones. Symptom reduction is seen as an end in itself.

Pharmacotherapy. The most commonly used group of antidepressant medications prescribed for children is the selective serotonin reuptake inhibitors (SSRIs). SSRIs influence the levels of serotonin (5-HT) in the brain. Evidence from randomized clinical trials suggests effectiveness in the treatment of moderate to severe depression in children and adolescents using three SSRIs: fluoxetine (Prozac), sertraline (Zoloft), and citalopram (Celexa).[15] Presently, fluoxetine is the only SSRI approved by the FDA to treat depression in children and adolescents (ages 8-18). In addition, the FDA has approved escitalopram (Lexapro) for the treatment of adolescent depression (12 and older). Any other medications used to treat depressive disorders in children or using an antidepressant in younger children is therefore considered an off-label use.

Suicide researcher Daniel Reidenberg suggests caution when using antidepressant medication in children and adolescents. He writes,

> There has been some concern that the use of antidepressant medications themselves may induce suicidal behavior in children and teens. Following a thorough and comprehensive review of all the available published and unpublished controlled clinical trials of antidepressants in children and adolescents, the FDA adopted a "black box" warning label in 2005 on all antidepressant medications to alert the public about the potential increased risk of suicidal thinking or attempts in children and adolescents taking antidepressants. In 2006, an advisory committee to the FDA recommended that the agency extend the warning to include young adults up to age 25.[16]

Because DMDD is such a new diagnosis, no treatment guidelines have been developed. However, several studies have shown that treatment with psychostimulants (e.g., Adderall) in children with comorbid ADHD and DMDD is effective in decreasing aggression. In cases of partial improvement, the addition of either risperidone (Risperdal) or divalproex (Depakote) appears to further decrease aggression. Children and adolescents with DMDD and marked aggression without ADHD may receive risperidone, as it appears to be the best studied treatment.[17]

Alex received therapy throughout his time in high school with little benefit. He continued to refuse the use of medication to treat his dysthymia. Richard said, "I regret not insisting he at least try the medication during high school. I was dealing with my own grief and wasn't fully aware of how seriously depressed he had become." In the fall after his senior year, Alex left for college. Richard said, "When I took him to campus, he threw a fit! He begged me to take him home and not make him stay. The next several weeks he called and texted constantly asking me to come and get him." At some point during his first semester, Alex simply stopped going to class. Soon after, his grandfather passed away and left him a large sum of money.

Alex left college and moved out of state to live in his grandfather's house. After six months, he moved back home and found an apartment not far from his father. Richard said, "Alex completely isolated himself. I would only hear from him occasionally." One afternoon Richard stopped by to visit Alex. "When he opened the door, the smell almost knocked me over. The apartment was a mess, and he was living with a large German shepherd. Dog feces and urine were everywhere. I couldn't believe what I was seeing." Richard called Alex's old therapist and asked if it would be possible have him committed to a psychiatric facility. The therapist told Richard that unless Alex was a danger to himself or others he could not be forcibly committed. Alex was evicted from the apartment two years later. After that Richard lost track of Alex for months at a time as he moved from place to place. Ultimately, he spent all his inheritance and had to move into his sister's garage.

A BIBLICAL PERSPECTIVE

While a number of individuals in the Scriptures, including King David and the prophets Jeremiah and Elijah, are described as suffering from the symptoms of depression, no description of a depressive disorder in a child or adolescent appears in the Old or New Testaments. However, a description of an adolescent struggling with depressive symptoms and suicidal thoughts does appear in the deuterocanonical book of Tobit.

The book of Tobit was written in the third or fourth century BC and describes events that occurred during the Assyrian captivity of the Israelite people (1 Chronicles 5:26; 2 Kings 15:29). One of the main characters of the book is a young woman named Sarah, the daughter of Raguel. Because Sarah and her family have been displaced by the Assyrians, she lives in Ecbatana, the capital of Media, in present-day Iran.

Although still a young woman, Sarah was a widower who had been married seven times. Mysteriously all of her husbands had died on their wedding night before the marriage could be consummated. The text tells us that the men were killed by the demon Asmodeus.[18] The demon was in love with Sarah and did not want anyone else to have her. Sarah, however, was not aware of Asmodeus's desire for her nor that he was the cause of her husbands' deaths. At the time of the events in the book of Tobit, Sarah is between seventeen and nineteen years old.

The deaths of her seven husbands had left Sarah broken, depressed, and shamed. As with most mental-health problems, Sarah's depression made it difficult for her to interact with people in a healthy way. The text tells us that out of her emotional distress she was mistreating her father's servants. In response to her abuse, the servants told Sarah they wished she was dead like her husbands and hoped she would never have children. For Sarah, this was the last straw. The sadness and shame were simply too much to live with; death was the only way out. Sarah decided to end her life, so she went to the upper room of her father's house to hang herself. As she prepared to take her life, she thought of the shame that her suicide would bring on her father. In Sarah's moment of desperation, her love for her father caused her to change plans. Rather than die by her own hand, she prayed that God would allow her to be released from this life.

God heard Sarah's prayer of desperation and sent the angel Raphael to heal her. Raphael brought a righteous kinsman of Sarah's family, Tobias, to become her husband. The angel then bound and imprisoned Asmodeus so he could no longer oppress Sarah. God blessed Sarah and Tobias with a long marriage and seven children.

The story of Sarah, daughter of Raguel emphasizes a foundational spiritual truth found throughout the Scriptures; God hears and answers our prayers. In her despair, Sarah cried out for God to take her life, much like Job did in the Old Testament (Job 3:1-26). Both believed death was the only way to stop their pain. God was not angered by the content of their prayers but rather drew near. In the case of Sarah, God understood that her distress required healing rather than simply spiritual deliverance (Tobit 3:17) and sent Raphael.

Unlike our limited view of the world, God's perspective is clear and complete. God knows we are easily overwhelmed by the difficult circumstances of our fallen world. He also understands that we often do not know what to pray. In Romans 8:26, Paul says, "In the same way the Spirit also helps our weakness; for we do not know how to pray as we should, but the Spirit Himself intercedes for us with groanings too deep for words." When we pray, we can rest in the fact that our imperfect requests and desperate pleas are intermingled with the perfect Words of the Holy Spirit and are received by God as fragrant incense (Psalm 141:2; Revelation 8:4). Sarah's desperate prayer for death began a spiritual process through which her life was restored, and she was drawn closer to the Healer. If a child is struggling with a mental disorder, cry out to God. Your prayers are heard! God is at work.

THE REST OF THE STORY

Now twenty-three, Alex has been employed at a local car dealership doing oil changes for the past year. Alex told his father that he is not happy with where he is in life, but he doesn't really remember what it is like to be happy. Recently, he agreed to try medication to treat his dysthymia. Richard said, "The change has been dramatic! He has only been on the medication for a little over a month, but I can already see that he is better. I have hope again for my son and his future." Alex is scheduled to start therapy with a new therapist in the next few weeks.

8

Emotional

Bipolar Disorders

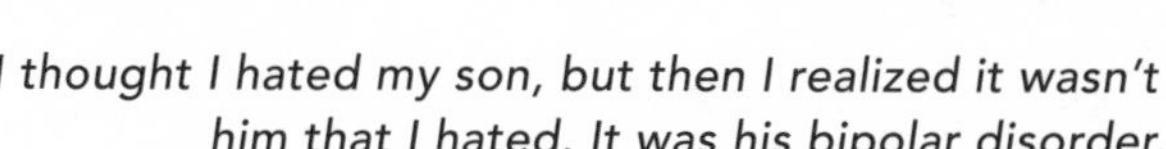

I thought I hated my son, but then I realized it wasn't him that I hated. It was his bipolar disorder.

STEPHANIE ESCAMILLA

UNABLE TO HAVE A CHILD on their own, Mark and Tiffany were overjoyed when the agency called them with the opportunity to adopt a one-day-old girl. They had only been on the adoption list for five months, and this seemed like a miracle. Lara was a blessing! Her birth mother reported no problems during the pregnancy, and she had a normal delivery. While the couple knew little about Lara's birth mother prior to the delivery, years later they would learn that she had a significant criminal history, primarily involving theft and check fraud.

Lara was a fussy baby, and her new mother struggled to care for her. Tiffany described Lara as "irritable and overly reactive" as a baby. While Lara crawled and walked on time, her speech development was delayed. Her pediatrician believed this was the result of a high palate, and Lara began speech therapy when she was two. Within a year, she began occupational therapy as well due to delayed fine-motor development. As Lara became a toddler, she began to show increasing problem behavior. Tiffany said she was oppositional and easily agitated. Her mood would change from minor irritability to an out of control temper tantrum with little provocation.

Lara began pre-kindergarten at a Christian school, and very early it was clear that she had significant learning deficits. In the next few years, she was found to have dyslexia, dysgraphia, and a specific math disorder.[1] Lara worked hard in school and with the help of tutors and an educational therapist was able to keep up. At home, however, her behavior had deteriorated to the point that Tiffany was afraid of her. Lara's temper tantrums no longer just involved kicking and screaming but also included throwing and breaking things as well as cursing. She was regularly lying and stealing from her parents. At one point during an anger outburst, she locked her parents out of the house. Tiffany made an appointment for Lara to have a neuropsychological assessment. Upon completing the battery of tests, seven-year-old Lara was diagnosed with ADHD (combined presentation). Tiffany was concerned about putting a seven year old on medication, and since the problem behaviors happened primarily at home, she felt that family therapy was their best option.

CHARACTERISTIC SYMPTOMS

Bipolar disorders are characterized by cycling mood changes. The affected child or adolescent alternates between severe highs (manic or hypomanic episodes) and severe lows (major depressive episodes), often with periods of normal mood in between. The mood changes can be rapid but most often occur gradually.

A *manic episode* is characterized by a distinct period of increased energy and abnormally elated, irritable, or euphoric mood that is present for most of the day, nearly every day, for at least one week. During the episode, three or more of the following symptoms (four or more if the mood is only irritable) must also be present: higher than usual self-esteem, significantly reduced need for sleep, an increase in talkativeness, racing thoughts, distractibility, an increase in goal-directed behavior (either socially, at work or school, or sexually) or psychomotor agitation, and excessive involvement in pleasurable activities that are risky or self-destructive (e.g., excessive spending, sexual promiscuity). Mania left untreated may worsen to a psychotic state.

A *hypomanic episode* is less intense and of shorter duration (at least four consecutive days) than a full manic episode. The most important differences between mania and hypomania are that the latter is not severe enough to cause marked impairment in daily functioning or to require hospitalization, and no psychotic features are present.

A *major depressive episode* (described in chap. 7) is characterized by either a persistent depressed mood or loss of interest or pleasure in daily activities over at least a two-week period.

DIAGNOSIS

In 1854, French psychiatrists Jules Baillarger and Jean-Pierre Falret made separate, independent presentations to the French Imperial Academy of Medicine in which they described a mental illness characterized by periodic shifts between mania and depression. Baillarger referred to this illness as "dual-form insanity" while Falret labeled it "circular insanity."[2] This marked the first appearance of bipolar disorder in psychiatric and medical literature. In 1899, the German psychiatrist Emil Kraepelin, expanding on Baillarger and Falret's earlier work, distinguished between two different forms of psychosis, manic-depressive psychosis (bipolar disorder) and dementia praecox (which would later become schizophrenia).[3] The term *manic-depressive illness* was used to describe the disorder until 1980 and the publication of the third edition of the *Diagnostic and Statistical Manual of Mental Disorders* (DSM-III), which introduced the term bipolar disorder.[4] In the most recent edition of the diagnostic manual, DSM-5, bipolar and related disorders are placed between the schizophrenia spectrum and other psychotic disorders and depressive disorders and serve as a bridge between these two diagnostic categories in terms of both symptoms and presentation. The primary bipolar disorders are bipolar I, bipolar II, and cyclothymia.

Bipolar I disorder is characterized by a manic episode that lasts at least seven days, severe enough to cause marked impairment in the child or adolescent's daily functioning, hospitalization to prevent harm to self or others, or the presences of psychotic symptoms. Usually, major depressive episodes occur as well.

Bipolar II disorder is characterized by a pattern of hypomanic and major depressive episodes, but the criterion for a full manic episode are not met. The hypomanic episode is associated with a clear change in daily functioning that is uncharacteristic of the individual.

Cyclothymic disorder (cyclothymia) is a milder form of bipolar disorder. Cyclothymic disorder is characterized by at least one year of periodic hypomanic and depressive symptoms. However, the symptoms do not meet the diagnostic criteria for any other type of bipolar disorder.

While descriptions of children and adolescents displaying what appears to be mania exist throughout antiquity, it was not until the 1980s that it became accepted for children and youth to be diagnosed with bipolar disorder.[5] Today, there is little disagreement that bipolar disorders exist in children. There is, however, significant disagreement in how the symptoms of bipolar disorder in children differ from those of adults. In younger children, chronic irritability and anger outbursts without mood swings are often seen. This troubled group of children has commonly been diagnosed with bipolar disorder even though they do not fully meet the DSM criteria for the disorder. To better classify this form of distress, the DSM-5 now includes the diagnosis of disruptive mood dysregulation disorder (DMDD).[6] In adolescents, where the presentation of bipolar disorder more closely resembles that of adults, there is much less controversy. In general, the older the child, the more the symptoms resemble those seen in adults. Existing evidence suggests that bipolar disorder beginning in childhood may be a different, possibly more severe, form of the illness than adolescent- and adult-onset bipolar disorder.

For Lara, a year of family therapy brought few positive results, so Tiffany sought a child psychiatrist. Lara tried two different ADHD medications, but both only made her irritability worse. The child psychiatrist questioned the ADHD diagnosis and felt that Lara's behavior was more consistent with pediatric (child-onset) bipolar disorder. Because the characteristic symptoms of ADHD, DMDD, and pediatric bipolar disorder overlap significantly, the misdiagnosis of children struggling with these disorders is not uncommon.

PREVALENCE AND AGE OF ONSET

The prevalence of pediatric (child-onset) bipolar disorder is not well established due to the debate about the definition of mania among pre-adolescents. In adolescents, however, the lifetime prevalence of bipolar disorders is well established.

Bipolar disorders occur in an estimated 2.9 percent of adolescents (13-18 years old). Among adolescents, a bipolar diagnosis appears to be more common in females than males.[7] The age of onset for the first manic, hypomanic, or major depressive episode is usually late adolescence to early adulthood, although it can occur at any age.

RISK FACTORS

The following factors have been shown to increase the risk of a child or adolescent being diagnosed with a bipolar disorder. Prenatal and perinatal risk factors include maternal viral infection, prenatal exposure to drugs (both prescribed medications and illegal drugs), extreme prematurity, and complications during labor and delivery.[8] Childhood risk factors include low socioeconomic status, parental mental illness, parental death or loss, emotional neglect, childhood physical/sexual abuse, seizure disorder, and attentional impairments (including a diagnosis of ADHD).[9] Higher rates of pediatric bipolar disorder have been found among children identified as having a difficult temperament during infancy, particularly those who display an inability to inhibit behavioral responses or have problems with emotional regulation. Lara showed several of these risk factors early in life. In addition to having a learning disorder with attentional problems, she was a temperamental infant and toddler: wildly impulsive and unable to control her emotions.

NEUROBIOLOGY

Heritability. Family studies find higher rates of bipolar disorder among the relatives of children diagnosed with pediatric bipolar than among the relatives of later-onset cases. These results suggest genetics may play a greater role in the pediatric form of bipolar disorder.[10] Twin studies looking at the role heredity plays in the bipolar disorders have found significantly higher concordance rates in identical twins (approximately 51 percent of twin pairs both have a bipolar disorder) compared to fraternal twins (approximately 6 percent share the disorder).[11]

Neuroanatomy. Neuroimaging studies of children and adolescents diagnosed with bipolar disorder have consistently demonstrated abnormalities in limbic areas of the brain, including the amygdala and hippocampus (an area involved in memory). In addition, children with bipolar disorder show reduced gray matter volumes in several areas of the brain, including the dorsolateral prefrontal cortex, temporal lobes, and cingulated gyrus. These results are consistent with those seen in adults diagnosed with bipolar disorder and suggest that disruption in a fronto-temporal pathway involved in the regulation of emotion is responsible for the mood dysregulation seen in bipolar disorder.[12]

Neurochemistry. Limited research has been done on the role of specific neurotransmitters in childhood bipolar disorder. However, several studies have shown decreased concentrations of glutamatergic metabolites in the brains of children who have been diagnosed with bipolar disorder compared to normal controls.[13] Glutamate is the most common excitatory neurotransmitter in the brain. Low levels of glutamate in the anterior cingulate cortex may be associated with the manic symptoms of childhood bipolar disorder.[14]

TREATMENT

The bipolar disorders are chronic, biologically driven problems that require medication for effective symptom management. Pharmacologic agents traditionally used to treat bipolar disorder in adults are increasingly prescribed for children and adolescents. Evidence supporting the effectiveness of these medications is increasing; however, significant gaps remain. Currently, there are no FDA-approved medications for treating bipolar disorders in children under age ten. In addition to medication, several forms of therapy have been shown to be effective in the treatment of bipolar disorders in children and adolescents.

Psychosocial treatment. Three therapeutic approaches have been shown to be effective in treating bipolar spectrum disorders in children and adolescents. Family-focused therapy (FFT) involves all members of a family or stepfamily and, in some cases, members of the extended family (e.g., grandparents). The goal of FFT is to help family members improve communication, learn effective problem-solving skills, understand and handle special family situations, enhance family coping strategies, and create a better functioning home environment. Family therapy is often combined with psychoeducation (PE). The principal goal of PE is to provide accurate and reliable information about the disorder, including ways of dealing with mental illness and its effects. Helping individuals to become more knowledgeable and aware of their disorder gives them more control over their condition. This awareness alone can help reduce the severity of symptoms and how often they occur.

A promising but as of yet experimental treatment is interpersonal and social rhythm therapy (IPSRT). IPSRT helps children with bipolar disorder identify and maintain the routines of everyday life. Regular daily routines and sleep schedules help protect against the onset of difficult symptoms. Resolving interpersonal issues and problems that may arise that directly impact the child's routines are also part of the therapy.[15]

Pharmacotherapy. Lithium was the first medication to be approved by the FDA for the treatment of mania in bipolar disorder for youth ages twelve to seventeen years. Unlike other medications used to treat mental disorders, lithium carbonate (e.g., Eskalith, Lithobid) is a salt, and consequently it does not have a specific receptor it binds to in the brain. Rather, after administration, lithium is widely distributed throughout the central nervous system, where it is transported into the brain's cells (neurons) through sodium channels in the cell membranes. Lithium appears to have a neuroprotective action by reestablishing chemical balance (homeostasis) in the neurons and decreasing their susceptibility to damage from both internal and external stimuli. Second, lithium promotes neurogenesis (the growth of new brain cells). This medication, while highly effective, has a number of serious side effects, and the range between an effective dose and a toxic dose is quite small.

A number of medications originally developed for treating seizure disorders have also been found to have mood-stabilizing affects. These include valproic acid or divalproex sodium (Depakote), lamotrigine (Lamictal), gabapentin (Neurontin), topiramate (Topamax), oxcarbazepine (Trileptal), and carbamazepine (Tegretol). These medications appear to exert their mood-stabilizing affects through a neuroprotective action similar to lithium. Anticonvulsant medications are most often used in combination with lithium, antidepressants, or atypical antipsychotics in the treatment of bipolar spectrum disorders. While these medications are regularly used to treat bipolar disorder in children and adolescents, none of them have been FDA-approved for that use in children.

The atypical antipsychotics modify the functioning of both dopamine and serotonin in the brain. These medications have been shown to have mood-stabilizing affects and are particularly useful for treating acute mania with or without psychotic symptoms. Atypical antipsychotics FDA-approved for the treatment of bipolar spectrum disorders in children and adolescents include olanzapine (Zyprexa; approved for

13-17 years old), aripiprazole (Abilify; approved for 10-17 years old), quetiapine (Seroquel; approved for 10-17 years old), risperidone (Risperdal; approved for 10-17 years old), and paliperidone (Invega; approved for 12-17 years old).[16]

With an accurate diagnosis of pediatric bipolar disorder, Lara was prescribed an atypical antipsychotic medication. Again, medication only made things worse. The psychiatrist suggested that Lara try a different medication. Tiffany had grown weary of medication's "empty promises" and instead enrolled the family in an intensive year-long family-focused therapy (FFT) program.

In this program, Lara received individual therapy, Tiffany and Mark worked with a therapist as a couple, and the whole family met together for therapy. Tiffany said that after a year, things were better at home, but Lara was still struggling. The family returned to the child psychiatrist hoping that since Lara was now older, she might respond better to medication. Ten-year-old Lara was prescribed a new medication, and Tiffany reports that last year was the best year they have ever had as a family.

A BIBLICAL PERSPECTIVE

The story of a frantic mother and a suffering young girl that appears in Matthew 15:21-28 and Mark 7:24-30 gives us a glimpse into the fear and desperation that comes when a child is diagnosed with a serious mental illness. To escape the constant questioning of the Jewish religious leaders, Jesus and his disciples traveled north of Galilee to Phoenicia and stayed in a home near the coastal cities of Tyre and Sidon. While he had tried to keep his presence in the region a secret, word of the famous Jewish rabbi with the power to heal the sick had reached the local people. Soon after his arrival, a desperate Gentile mother whose young daughter was afflicted by an evil spirit sought Jesus.

In Jesus' time, madness (mental illness) was thought to be associated with the work of demons. We see this illustrated in Jesus' own life when he is accused on multiple occasions of being both insane and possessed by a demon (Mark 3:21-22, 30-31; John 7:20; 8:48, 52; 10:19-20). Because the people of Jesus' time believed demonic possession was the cause of insanity, we can be fairly confident that the woman's daughter was suffering from some form of developmental or psychiatric illness.

Her daughter was not just ill but strange—perhaps struggling with delusions or violent outbursts. When the woman found Jesus, she fell at his feet and begged him to help her suffering child. In the culture of the day, it was improper for a woman to directly address a man, but cultural norms were not going to stand in the way of this loving mother finding help for her tormented child. Initially, Jesus ignores her and does not respond. He intentionally waits until the disciples, weary of her pleas and violations of their social boundaries, ask him to send her away.

Jesus' response to the woman is harsh and offensive, typical of what she would have received from any Jewish man of the day. He tells her that he was sent to the children of Israel and not to unclean Gentiles such as herself. He even refers to her as a "little dog," a common ethnic slur of the day used by Jews when referring to those outside the covenant. Despite Jesus' hurtful statement, the woman is not put off. She reminds him that even "little dogs" benefit when the children of a family are blessed because they receive the "crumbs" that fall from the family's table.

The true reason for Jesus' presence in a Gentile land and his harsh response to the desperate woman becomes clear as he compliments the woman for the depth of her faith. The trip and the cruel response had all been an opportunity for Jesus to teach his disciples that the Messianic grace being offered to the Jews would overflow far beyond Israel and bless even the pagan Gentiles. He then tells her to return home because her daughter had been healed. Overwhelmed with emotion, the woman quickly made her way home to find her young daughter resting in bed completely healed, just as Jesus had said.

Before she approached Jesus, the woman had likely sought other physicians and "healers" in a desperate attempt to cure her suffering daughter. She simply would not give up on her child; no distance was too far to walk, no situation too personally humiliating, no price too high to pay, no cultural boundary too strong to break. A diagnosis of childhood bipolar disorder may seem like a burden that a parent simply cannot carry, but your child needs you to be unrelenting. To empower us to overcome hardships in this world, God has called us to stay connected to him through prayer. In the parable of the persistent widow, Jesus teaches us that regardless of how hopeless the circumstances may appear; we should pray and never give up (Luke 18:1-8). Paul emphasizes this teaching of Jesus in 1 Thessalonians 5:17 when he writes, "pray without ceasing." God wants to walk through difficult times with parents and their child. As we seek healing for a child, Jesus simply asks that we also seek his comfort and guidance so we might be able to persevere.

THE REST OF THE STORY

As twelve-year-old Lara prepares to begin the sixth grade this year, her family is more hopeful than ever. Tiffany says that strangely there is a "silver lining" to Lara's bipolar disorder. "She is very independent and outspoken, but in a good way. She makes friends easily. Teachers adore her! She loves sports and is a competitive gymnast." While Lara makes friends easily, they often feel her wrath when she becomes upset, and as a result she has damaged relationships. Tiffany said, "Lara's problems have brought Mark and me closer together as a couple, but if I'm being honest, we are both exhausted and stressed most of the time. We work hard to stay on the same page when it comes to our daughter. I believe everything happens for a reason. I feel blessed that Lara was given to us. We have been able to get her the help she needs. I'm not sure her birth mother would have been able to do that."

I asked Tiffany what advice she would give a mother with a child in a similar situation. "Don't worry about the diagnosis, focus on the behavior. What are the core behaviors that are a problem? Ask yourself, 'how can I help the behavior?'"

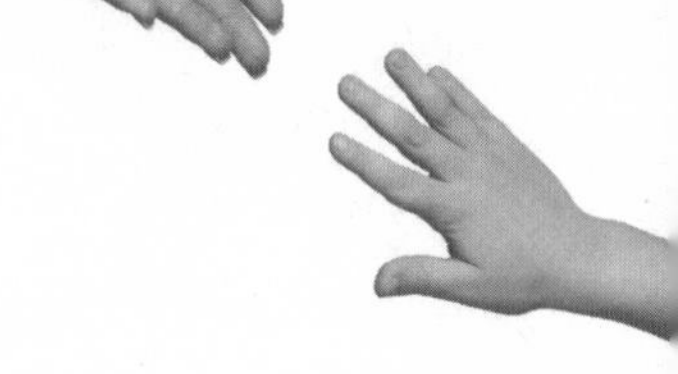

9

Fearful

Anxiety Disorders

It was scary to listen to my daughter share her anxious thoughts.

KAMI GILMORE

IN MANY WAYS Tim is your typical nine-year-old boy. He loves history, Nerf guns, hikes in the woods, and minibikes. However, his mother Christy said, "He has always been an anxious child. He is very cautious and overthinks everything." While Tim's anxiety has always been present, it did not really become a problem until he started the second grade. Christy said, "He would cry and not want to go to school. Many times I had to go and sit in his classroom to get him to go to school. He was constantly 'sick' with headaches, nausea, or diarrhea. He worried about everything. He started sleeping in his clothes just in case there was a hurricane, or a fire, or some catastrophe." Christy met with Tim's teacher, but neither was sure what to do. Things became worse when Tim, sick to his stomach, wasn't able to make it to the restroom and threw up in the school hallway. "Ever since the vomiting incident at school, he has been terrified that he is going to throw up in public. It's one more reason he worries and doesn't want to leave the house."

CHARACTERISTIC SYMPTOMS

An anxiety disorder is a condition experienced both mentally and physically. It causes children to feel that there are things they cannot control, fear various problems that may not even exist, and worry about things more than they deserve. The characteristic symptoms of these disorders are persistent irrational fear or anxiety and panic attacks.

Irrational fear or *anxiety* is an overwhelming, disruptive feeling of dread far out of proportion to the actual risk. The child or adolescent may recognize this fear is excessive and unreasonable, yet is unable to calm themselves. "*Fear* is the emotional response to the real or perceived imminent threat, whereas *anxiety* is the anticipation of future threat. . . . The anxiety disorders differ from one another by the types of objects or situations that induce fear, anxiety, or avoidance behavior."[1]

A *panic attack* is a sudden surge of overwhelming fear and anxiety that reaches a peak within minutes. The DSM-5 lists thirteen potential symptoms of a panic attack: increased heart rate, sweating, trembling, shortness of breath, feelings of choking, chest pain, nausea, dizziness, chills or heat sensations, numbness or tingling, feelings of unreality or depersonalization (being detached from oneself), fear of losing control, or fear of dying. Four or more of these symptoms must be present for the episode to be considered a panic attack. A panic attack may be a one-time occurrence in an individual's life, but many children with an anxiety disorder experience multiple episodes.

DIAGNOSIS

While severe anxiety has been recognized as a problem since antiquity, it was typically considered only a symptom of melancholia. This is understandable because even modern mental-health-care providers seldom encounter seriously depressed patients who are not also anxious to a significant degree.[2] While the first modern medical description of anxiety appeared in Richard Burton's 1621 compendium *The Anatomy of Melancholia*, it was not until 1980 and the publication of DSM-III that a diagnostic system to identify anxiety disorders with a childhood onset was available to mental-health-care providers.

In the DSM-5, the section on anxiety disorders is placed immediately after the depressive disorders, recognizing the strong relationship between these two categories of distress. The primary anxiety disorders are separation anxiety disorder, selective mutism, specific phobia, social anxiety disorder, panic disorder, agoraphobia, and generalized anxiety disorder.

Separation anxiety disorder is characterized by inappropriate and excessive fear or anxiety concerning separation from home or those the child is attached to. The fear or anxiety is persistent, lasting at least four weeks in children and adolescents.

Selective mutism is characterized by an inability to speak in some social settings and to some people for at least one month. A child with selective mutism may talk normally at home or when alone with parents, but cannot speak at all or above a whisper in other social settings. The disorder is often marked by high social anxiety.

Specific phobia is characterized by extreme and irrational fear or anxiety about a specific object or situation. Specific phobias commonly focus on animals, insects, germs, heights, thunder, driving, public transportation, flying, dental or medical procedures, and elevators.

Social anxiety disorder is characterized by marked fear or anxiety about social situations in which the child or adolescent is exposed to possible scrutiny or judgment by others. The fear or anxiety causes clinically significant distress lasting for six months or more.

Panic disorder is characterized by recurrent panic attacks that strike suddenly and without warning. Children with panic disorder often develop intense anxiety between episodes, worrying about when and where the next panic attack will occur. To compensate for this anxiety, panic-disordered individuals often begin to avoid places and situations where they have experienced an attack. Some children's lives become so restricted that they avoid even everyday activities such as going to school.

Agoraphobia is characterized by the avoidance of situations or places where the person thinks escape might be difficult or help might be unavailable in the event of a panic attack or other incapacitating or embarrassing symptoms.

Generalized anxiety disorder (GAD) is characterized by excessive anxiety and worry, even though there is little or nothing to provoke it, occurring for at least six months. In GAD, the anxiety is severe enough to affect the child or adolescent's ability to function daily. The anxiety is always more intense than the situation warrants, and the child will often recognize it as such. With GAD, the anxiety is accompanied by at least three physical symptoms such as fatigue, sleeplessness, headache, muscle tension, sweating, shortness of breath, irritability, and hot flashes. During the course of the disorder, the focus of worry may shift from one concern to another.

Christy recognized that Tim's fears had become overwhelming. For example, "When he would see a roach, he would scream and start taking off his clothes because he was convinced the roach was on him even though he could still see it on the floor." He was irritable, had trouble sleeping, constantly washed his hands, and was always "sick." Christy scheduled an appointment for Tim to be assessed by a child psychologist who diagnosed him with generalized anxiety disorder.

PREVALENCE AND AGE OF ONSET

Anxiety disorders are the most common mental disorders in children and adolescents. The lifetime prevalence of any anxiety disorder in children or adolescents is estimated to be 15-20 percent of the population. The age of onset of selective mutism is usually before five years, while separation anxiety disorder, specific phobia, and social anxiety disorder usually first manifest in later childhood. Panic disorder, agoraphobia, and GAD typically have their onset in later adolescence to early adulthood. Tim, however, was only eight when he was diagnosed with GAD.

The most common anxiety disorders among children and adolescents are specific phobias (11 percent), social anxiety disorder (7 percent), and separation anxiety disorder (3 percent). Selective mutism (less than 1 percent) is the least common of the anxiety disorders. Agoraphobia and panic disorder show a low prevalence during childhood (less than 1 percent); higher prevalence rates are found in adolescence (2-3 percent). The prevalence rate for GAD among adolescents is 1 percent. In childhood, anxiety disorders occur equally in boys and girls, but after puberty, prevalence rates increase to a ratio of 2:1 (female-male).[3]

RISK FACTORS

Like all mental illnesses, anxiety disorders result from a complex interaction of psychosocial, biological, and developmental factors. Since the 1950s, research has shown a significant increase in the anxiety levels of children, teens, and college students.[4] This increase is associated with a lack of social connection and a sense of a more threatening environment. Prenatal and perinatal risk factors for anxiety disorders include maternal psychological distress, prenatal alcohol exposure, and a low Apgar score. Tim's mother, Christy, struggles with severe anxiety, and because she refused to take medication while pregnant, she dealt with significant psychological distress and panic attacks while carrying Tim.

Early childhood events such as trauma, poverty, a negative family environment, death of a parent or sibling, and academic failure appear to be predisposing factors.[5] Major life stressors such as a physical illness, divorce, or a move to a new home or school may also play a role in triggering the onset of an anxiety disorder. Psychological factors such as low self-esteem, fear of being abandoned or rejected, feelings of intense loneliness and helplessness, and early onset depression have all been shown to increase the risk for developing a childhood anxiety disorder.

NEUROBIOLOGY

Heritability. Studies using twin pairs have consistently found higher concordance rates for the anxiety disorders in identical (monozygotic) twins when compared to fraternal (dizygotic) twins.[6] The contribution of genetic factors is estimated to be 73 percent for separation anxiety disorder, 67 percent for agoraphobia, 51 percent for social anxiety disorder, 48 percent for panic disorder, 32 percent for GAD and 30 percent for specific phobias. Panic disorder, generalized anxiety disorder, and specific phobias have all been found to have a significantly higher rate of occurrence in first-degree relatives of patients with anxiety disorders.[7]

Neuroanatomy. Brain imaging studies in children and adolescents with anxiety disorders have found abnormalities in several brain areas related to fear and stress. These areas include the prefrontal cortex (PFC), amygdala, and anterior cingulate gyrus.[8] These brain areas are all part of a neural pathway that assesses the threat level of situations, objects, and events. This system also activates the fight-or-flight response as the body prepares itself for danger. This stress response is what triggers symptoms like sweating and a pounding heart when we are afraid or anxious. When this system is not functioning correctly, a child may experience high levels of anxiety in situations that are not stressful or pose no threat. This inability to effectively assess the level of threat related to everyday situations leads to the development of an anxiety disorder.

Neurochemistry. Limited research literature exists on the role of specific neurotransmitters in the development of child and adolescent anxiety disorders. However, the few studies that have been done clearly demonstrate that increased activity in the norepinephrine (NE) neurotransmitter system is associated with anxiety disorders in children and adolescents.[9] Having too much NE can cause irritability, high blood pressure, excessive sweating, heart palpitations, and headaches. All of which are common symptoms in panic attacks.

TREATMENT

While anxiety disorders are the most commonly diagnosed mental illnesses in children and adolescents, they are also the most treatable. When left untreated, they put children at risk for major depression and substance abuse in late adolescence and adulthood. As with most mental disorders, a combined treatment approach using both therapy and medication is found to be most effective.

Behavioral therapy. The therapeutic approach shown to be most effective in treating anxiety disorders is cognitive-behavioral therapy (CBT). In CBT the clinician teaches the child adaptive coping skills and provides practice opportunities to develop a sense of mastery over anxiety symptoms or situations that are associated with distress. The most widely used and best-researched CBT protocol for youths (ages 7–14) is the Coping Cat Program. The Coping Cat Program involves multiple sixty-minute sessions over a twelve- to sixteen-week period. The first half of the sessions focus on learning new skills, and the second half of the sessions give the child an opportunity to practice the newly learned skills both within the sessions and in real life. Research has demonstrated that parent involvement improves CBT treatment outcome in anxious children and teens. Parents are seen as collaborators and consultants in the child's treatment and are given a model for assisting with the treatment in the role of the child's CBT coach.[10]

Pharmacotherapy. Presently no selective serotonin reuptake inhibitor (SSRI) is FDA approved for treating anxiety disorders in children and adolescents, although they are often prescribed off-label for this use. The only medication approved by the FDA for the treatment of generalized anxiety disorder in children is the selective serotonin and norepinephrine reuptake inhibitor (SNRI) duloxetine (Cymbalta; seven years and up). SNRIs increase the levels of both serotonin (5-HT) and norepinephrine (NE) in the brain. There is an increased risk of suicidal thinking and behavior in children and adolescents taking antidepressant medications, a risk that should always be weighed against the potential benefits of the medication.

Benzodiazepines are prescribed less often than SNRIs or SSRIs for children but can be used to treat acute anxiety such as panic attacks that interfere with a child's ability to carry out everyday activities. This class of drugs is used for short-term treatment. Benzodiazepines work by affecting the activity of the brain neurotransmitter gamma-aminobutyric acid (GABA). By enhancing the action of GABA, benzodiazepines have a calming effect on parts of the brain that are too excitable. Examples of benzodiazepines include lorazepam (Ativan), clonazepam (Klonopin), diazepam (Valium), and alprazolam (Xanax). Children can build up a tolerance to these medications and may require increased doses to experience the same effects.[11]

Once diagnosed with GAD, Tim began meeting weekly with a therapist, and a child psychiatrist prescribed two medications: one for anxiety and another to help his attention. The combination of therapy and medication worked. Christy saw a clear reduction in Tim's anxiety. He still struggled, but he was better. As Tim continued to improve, he was able to reduce the number of times he met with his therapist from once a week to once a month. He was also able to develop a number of coping behaviors to help control his anxiety. "When he feels his anxiety coming on, he will put essential oils on himself." Christy carries them in her purse. He also has a blanket that brings him comfort as well as a stress ball (a balloon filled with Play-Doh) that he always keeps in his pocket.

Tim had improved so much that the summer after third grade Christy wanted to see how he would do without the medication. At his mother's request, Tim was weaned off the medication by the psychiatrist. Christy described the experience as a "horrible mistake." Almost immediately, Tim's anxiety became overwhelming. All the progress he had made was gone, and he was quickly placed back on the medication. Several weeks have passed since Tim restarted the medication, and while his anxiety has decreased, Christy says, "His anxiety is not as well controlled as it was before we stopped the medication."

A BIBLICAL PERSPECTIVE

Anxiety is a common topic in the Scriptures. We find it discussed throughout the wisdom literature (Job, Psalms,

Proverbs, and Ecclesiastes), by Jesus in the Gospels (Matthew and Luke), and in the epistles of Paul (Philippians) and Peter (1 Peter). We also see it manifested in the lives of many Old Testament and New Testament biblical characters including Adam, Job, Saul, David, Elijah, Martha, Paul, and Peter. I'm not suggesting that any of these people had an anxiety disorder, but they, like all of us, had times when they struggled with fear and worry.

In the Scriptures, both the Hebrew (*sar'aph* [e.g., Psalm 94:19]) and Greek (*merimnaō* [Philippians 4:6]) words we translate as "anxious" have their origins in words meaning "division" or "to separate into parts." That's what unhealthy levels of anxiety do, divide our thoughts. The biblical authors also recognized that fear and anxiety had both cognitive (mental) and physiological (physical) components. A number of Scriptures describe the mental anguish of anxiety (e.g., Psalm 94:19; Proverbs 12:25), while others illustrate that overwhelming fear can cause a pounding heart, trembling, and physical pain (Job 4:14; Psalm 48:5-6; Isaiah 13:7-8; 21:3-4; Sirach 48:19).

Anxiety at normal levels is healthy. Concern for the well-being of others or a physiological response that rouses us to action in a threatening or dangerous situation is a God-given part of our being. But an anxiety disorder is destructive both physically and spiritually. Children and adolescents with anxiety disorders are often so focused on trying to control their circumstances to avoid some potential threat or catastrophe that they begin to perceive God as a punitive task master. He is seen as someone who can never be satisfied no matter how hard they try. When ministering to children with anxiety, we must remind them that because of God's grace and forgiveness we do not have to perform for his love and acceptance, we already have it if we are in Christ (2 Corinthians 5:17).

The bodies and brains of children suffering from anxiety disorders are wired to be anxious. Neither of the following two practices will relieve the mental and physical distress associated with an anxiety disorder: simply quoting Philippians 4:6: "Be anxious for nothing, but in everything by prayer and supplication with thanksgiving let your requests be made known to God," or memorizing Isaiah 41:10 (NIV):

> So do not fear, for I am with you;
> do not be dismayed, for I am your God.
> I will strengthen you and help you;
> I will uphold you with my righteous right hand.

Rather, to correct their misperceptions of God's character and build a foundation for recovery, you can gently lead them back to Scriptures that describe God's good nature (e.g., "Gracious is the LORD, and righteous; Yes, our God is compassionate" [Psalm 116:5]) and who we are in Christ ("As many as received Him, to them He gave the right to become children of God, *even* to those who believe in His name" [John 1:12]). As the psalmist writes, "When my anxious thoughts multiply within me, Your consolations delight my soul" (Psalm 94:19).

THE REST OF THE STORY

To try to help his anxiety, Tim's parents have decided to move him to a public school next year. Christy explained, "The small Christian school that he attends has an accelerated curriculum, and the academic expectations are very high. That only adds to his anxiety." Tim is worried about going to a new school, so Christy is trying to lessen his fears by taking him on bike trips to visit the school during the summer so he might see it as a safe place. I asked Christy how this experience has affected her faith. She said, "I struggle with severe anxiety myself, and I find that when my anxiety is at its worst, I draw closer to God. I read the Bible more and pray more during those times. It brings me great comfort and peace. I'm trying to teach that to Tim."

10

Wounded

Posttraumatic Stress Disorder

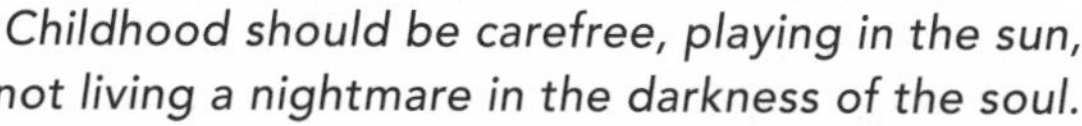

Childhood should be carefree, playing in the sun, not living a nightmare in the darkness of the soul.

DAVE PELZER

When Jana and her family went to bed on Saturday night, they had no idea that their lives were about to change. While they had been watching the weather reports throughout the previous week, they did not expect that the approaching hurricane would affect them. They lived fifty miles from the coast in an area that historically had never flooded. Hurricane Harvey, however, was no ordinary hurricane. After the storm made landfall south of Houston, it stalled just inland for the next two days, dropping heavy rainfall and causing widespread flooding. Jana said,

> We live along one of the major bayous that runs through the city. My husband noticed that the water was rising,

> but I still didn't think it would reach our house. I've never seen water move like that. One minute it was at the edge of our backyard, and the next minute it was rushing in the backdoor. Within minutes, there was three feet of water in our house, and it was still rising. We grabbed our three kids and waded through four or five feet of water to a neighbor's home. By the time it was all over there was more than six feet of water in our house.

The next day, the family stayed in a shelter, and that is when Jana first noticed that her eight-year-old son, Duncan, was struggling. "He was very clingy, but I dismissed it because it was a strange place and a lot had happened. I didn't think too much of it. Later he woke up because he wet the bed. He had never had problems with bed-wetting before." Over the next few days Duncan would never leave Jana's side. Once the water receded, he refused to return to the home to survey the damage, which meant that Jana could not go either. When she suggested he stay with his Dad while she went to the house, he began to cry uncontrollably.

CHARACTERISTIC SYMPTOMS

Posttraumatic stress disorder (PTSD) is characterized by significant psychological distress lasting more than a month following exposure to a potentially life-threatening (or perceived life-threatening) traumatic event such as childhood neglect, childhood physical or sexual abuse, war, physical assault, sexual assault, domestic violence, natural disaster, serious illness, or an accident. The traumatic event overwhelms the child's ability to cope, both cognitively and physiologically, leaving them feeling as if the world is an unsafe, dangerous, and out-of-control place. In some sense the child becomes trapped in the traumatic experience and is unable to move forward, as evidenced by the following symptoms.

Intrusion symptoms include recurrent, involuntary, and distressing memories, thoughts, and dreams of the traumatic event. In children these intrusive memories may not necessarily appear distressing and may be expressed as play reenactment. For children's distressing dreams, it may not be possible to determine that the frightening content is specifically related to the traumatic event. Exposure to stimuli or cues that resemble some aspect of the traumatic event may also result in marked distress for the child.

Avoidance symptoms are efforts to avoid internal (memories, thoughts, feelings) or external (people, places, situations) reminders of the traumatic event. Preoccupation with avoiding trauma-related feelings and stimuli can become a central focus of the child's life.

Negative alterations in cognition and mood include an increased frequency of fear, guilt, sadness, shame, and confusion. A markedly diminished interest in activities previously considered pleasurable often results in the child becoming socially withdrawn and isolated.

Hyper-arousal symptoms are often reported to be some of the most troubling symptoms of PTSD. These symptoms include being jumpy and easily startled, irritability, temper outbursts, self-destructive behavior, problems concentrating, and difficulty sleeping. Teens are more likely than younger children to show impulsive and aggressive behaviors.

DIAGNOSIS

While it was long doubted that children could develop PTSD, this is no longer debatable. In the days and weeks following a traumatic experience, most children will show some of the symptoms described in the previous section. In the context of diagnosis, two factors are important to consider: (1) the duration of the symptoms and (2) the severity of the distress; is there a clinically significant disturbance in the child's functioning? A PTSD diagnosis cannot be given until symptoms have lasted for more than one month. Children and teens who display clinically significant impairment within the first month following a traumatic event are often given a diagnosis of acute stress disorder (ASD). ASD is similar to PTSD, but the duration of the psychological distress last only three days to one month following exposure to the traumatic event. The symptoms that define ASD overlap with those for PTSD.[1]

The DSM-I published in 1952 included the diagnosis of gross stress reaction. The criteria for this disorder were intentionally broad and recognized that exposure to traumatic events other than combat (e.g., natural disaster) could also cause significant distress. Gross stress reaction was combined with adjustment disorder in the DSM-II, published in 1968, and referred to as adjustment reaction of adult life. The publication of the DSM-III in 1980 saw the inclusion of post-traumatic stress disorder for the first time. PTSD was listed as one of the anxiety disorders. Subsequent editions of the diagnostics manual (DSM-III-R, DSM-IV, DSM-IV-TR) continued to include PTSD as an anxiety disorder.[2]

It wasn't until the publication of the DSM-III-R in 1987 that special developmental considerations for children and adolescents were added to the PTSD criteria. In the most recent edition of the manual, DSM-5, all trauma- and stressor-related disorders, including PTSD and ASD, are for the first time grouped together in a single category. DSM-5 also includes a new developmental subtype of PTSD called posttraumatic stress disorder in preschool children (6 and younger).

Jana's family found an apartment to rent while their house was being repaired, but Duncan's fear only grew worse. Jana said,

> He refused to sleep in his room and insisted on sleeping on the floor next to our bed. He always slept in his clothes and kept a backpack full of clothes and toys nearby just in case we had to run again. He had trouble sleeping, and when he did fall asleep he would often wake up because of nightmares. He also continued to

wet the bed. If it rained, he would become physically ill with nausea and headaches.

After several weeks with no improvement Jana made an appointment for Duncan with a child psychologist. Duncan was diagnosed with posttraumatic stress disorder.

PREVALENCE AND AGE OF ONSET

PTSD can occur at any age. Determining the prevalence of PTSD is somewhat difficult because unlike other mental disorders, it does not spontaneously occur. Instead, it is triggered by exposure to a specific traumatic event. Research finds that about 15–43 percent of children and teens will experience at least one trauma.[3] The lifetime prevalence of PTSD in adolescents (13–18 years old) is estimated to be 5 percent of the population. Prevalence rates of PTSD are higher for girls than boys.[4] There are no definitive studies on prevalence rates of PTSD in younger children in the general population.

RISK FACTORS

A number of factors have been found to increase a child's risk of significant distress following exposure to a traumatic event. Prenatal and perinatal risk factors include maternal psychological distress and low IQ. Early childhood risk factors include previous trauma exposure, preexisting psychological disorders, parental mental illness, lower socioeconomic status, high trait anxiety, and low social support.[5] Several factors associated with the traumatic experience itself have also been shown to influence whether a child will manifest PTSD. These include the severity of the trauma and how close or far away the child is from the trauma. For example, events that involve people hurting other people, such as rape and assault, are more likely to result in PTSD than other types of traumas.

NEUROBIOLOGY

Heritability. Like all mental disorders, PTSD would be considered a polygenetic disorder. This means the disorder does not result from variation in a single gene but rather a child's inherited vulnerability for PTSD is likely influenced by multiple genes. Family studies demonstrate that children whose mother or father has been diagnosed with PTSD are five times more likely to receive the diagnosis themselves compared to children whose parents did not develop PTSD.[6] Twins studies have found that 30–40 percent of the variance in PTSD symptoms can be accounted for by genetic factors.[7] Taken together these data indicate that the genetic makeup of some children renders them considerably more vulnerable than others to developing distressing symptoms following trauma.

Neuroanatomy. Exposure to trauma during childhood can have devastating effects on the developing brain. Brain-imaging research has found that children with PTSD, when compared to normal controls, show smaller total brain volumes and abnormalities in the prefrontal cortex, right temporal lobe, prefrontal cortical white matter, and corpus callosum. Several studies have also found that early trauma exposure effects the maturation of the amygdala and hippocampus.[8] These two deep brain structures are part of the limbic system and are involved in the assessment of threat and the experience of fear. These studies demonstrate that childhood PTSD is associated with adverse brain development and places the child at significant risk for mental-health problems later in adulthood.

Neurochemistry. Research has shown that the tremendous increases in neurotransmitter activity seen with severe or prolonged trauma have a significant impact on brain development. Children with PTSD as a result of maltreatment show evidence of increased catecholamine (specifically norepinephrine) and cortisol activity. In a normal child, fear or anxiety activates the locus coeruleus, the major norepinephrine-containing nucleus in the brain, and the sympathetic nervous system, causing the adrenal glands to release the glucocorticoid cortisol. These neurochemical changes generate a fight-or-flight stress response. In the traumatized child, this stress response is overactive, resulting in physiological problems (e.g., increased blood pressure) and brain-cell death due to the neurotoxicity of high levels of glucocorticoids. Similar dysregulation has been shown in adults diagnosed with PTSD.[9]

TREATMENT

The parents of children who have experienced a traumatic event should seek a comprehensive psychological assessment for their child as soon as they note symptoms of PTSD. Early detection and intervention is important and can reduce the severity of symptoms, enhance the child's normal growth and development, and improve the child's overall quality of life.

Psychosocial treatment. Trauma-focused cognitive behavioral therapy (TF-CBT) is the most effective therapeutic technique for treating children and adolescents with PTSD. In TF-CBT, children learn new skills to help manage and resolve distressing thoughts, feelings, and behaviors related to the trauma. This therapeutic approach also includes techniques to help reduce worry and stress. TF-CBT can be used with children and adolescents who have experienced a single trauma or multiple traumas in their life.

Eye movement desensitization and reprocessing (EMDR) has also been shown to be effective in treating PTSD in children and adolescents. EMDR combines aspects of cognitive therapy with directed eye movements. During an EMDR session the therapist moves her fingers back and forth in front of the child's face while asking them to follow her hand motions with their eyes. At the same time the therapist has the child recall distressing events related to the traumatic experience. This includes the emotions and body sensations that go along with it. Gradually, the therapist helps the child shift their thoughts to more pleasant ones. Unlike in TF-CBT, the child is not required to talk about or openly discuss the traumatic experience. Studies have shown that eye movements are not necessary for EMDR to be effective.

Play therapy can be used to treat young children who do not have the cognitive abilities and verbal skills to deal with trauma directly. In play therapy, the therapist uses games, drawing, painting, and other play-related methods to help the child express and process their traumatic memories.[10]

Duncan began meeting weekly with a therapist for TF-CBT. Several weeks later when school restarted, Duncan found it difficult to concentrate and struggled to keep up with his peers. Jana said, "That was a tough semester for Duncan, but we made it. It took about two months of weekly therapy before I started to notice an improvement in him."

Pharmacotherapy. The present research data does not support the use of medication as a first-line treatment for PTSD in children and adolescents. However, SSRIs (e.g., Zoloft), antiadrenergic agents (e.g., Catapres), atypical antipsychotics (e.g., Risperdal), and mood stabilizers (e.g., Tegretol) may be helpful when used for specific PTSD symptoms. Currently, no medication is FDA-approved for the treatment of PTSD in the pediatric population.[11]

A BIBLICAL PERSPECTIVE

Traumatic events such as murder (Genesis 4:8), family abandonment (Genesis 21:14), famine (Genesis 41:54), war (Joshua 6:20), rape (Judges 19:25), natural disasters (Jeremiah 14:4), deadly accidents (Luke 13:4), and physical assault (2 Corinthians 11:25) are common human experiences that existed in biblical times as well as today. The Scriptures give details of several adolescents who experienced significant trauma. These include the rape of Dinah (Genesis 34:2) and the assault and enslavement of Joseph (Genesis 37:23-24, 28). The most detailed account of adolescent trauma, however, is found in the story of Tamar.

Tamar was the daughter of King David and Maacah; she was the sister of Absalom. An unmarried virgin between thirteen and fifteen years old, she is described as more beautiful than all the other women of the kingdom. The book of 2 Samuel and the writings of the first-century Roman-Jewish historian Titus Flavius Josephus provide details of Tamar's rape.[12]

The Scriptures tell us that Amnon, King David's eldest son and heir to the Israelite throne, developed an unnatural romantic obsession with his young half-sister. However, marriage between half-siblings was forbidden by the law (Leviticus 18:11). In addition, Tamar was a virgin princess and likely had a marriage arranged for her with a young prince in a neighboring kingdom. This was a common practice in biblical times; marriage to a royal princess was used to strengthen alliances between neighboring rulers. Tamar's own mother, Maacah, was the daughter of Talmai, king of Geshur, and had been given to David in marriage for just that purpose. Amnon became so lovesick for Tamar that he stopped eating and began to lose weight.

Jonadab, Amnon's cousin and friend, was not an honorable man. The Scriptures describe him as "shrewd" and "crafty." Jonadab devised a plan so that Amnon could get Tamar alone and fulfill his lustful obsession. Amnon feigned illness and asked his father King David to send Tamar to his house to make him a special meal to help him recover. David immediately called for Tamar. Once she had prepared the meal, Amnon sent his guards and attendants away, leaving him and Tamar alone in his bed chamber. Amnon, lying on his bed "ill" and "weak," asked her to feed him the cakes she had prepared. Once she was near, he grabbed her and tried to seduce her into sleeping with him. Tamar resisted, recognizing the sinfulness of the act. She tried to reason with her half-brother and begged him to ask their father for his approval to marry. While marriage between half-siblings was forbidden by the law, it was a common practice in neighboring nations. King David would likely not have denied his firstborn son's request. Amnon would not listen. He overpowered Tamar and raped her.

Once the brutal act was over, Amnon, disgusted by the sight of Tamar lying on the bed, bloodied and bruised, ordered her to leave. Again the young princess pleaded with her half-brother. To send her away a violated woman was worse than raping her. She would never be able to marry or have children. In the culture of the day, her life was over. Having dishonored her, the law required that Amnon now marry her to save her reputation (Deuteronomy 22:28-29). Amnon would not listen. He ordered his attendants to throw Tamar out.

The world had changed for Tamar. Weeping she put ashes on her head as a sign of mourning. She tore the ceremonial gown identifying her as a royal virgin and covered her head with her hand as a sign of shame. Absalom, her brother, tried to comfort her but only increased her shame and pain by instructing her not to tell anyone what had happened. When King David heard what Amnon had done, he was angry but did nothing. Absalom, a concerned brother, moved Tamar out of the king's harem and into his house. There, the Scriptures say, she lived out her days "desolate."

From that point forward, Absalom looked for an opportunity to avenge his sister. Two years later, Absalom had his servants kill Amnon in front of all their brothers during a banquet at his home. To honor his shamed sister, Absalom later named his own daughter Tamar.

Survivors of trauma tend to heal and recover faster when they are in a supportive community. Social connection and engagement help survivors and their families feel they are cared for and know that they are not alone. Absalom honored his traumatized sister by bringing her into his house rather than sending her away to live on the fringes of society. He blessed her with a niece named in her honor and made sure her rapist was held accountable according to the Mosaic law. While I am in no way advocating violence or vigilant justice, faith communities share a divine responsibility to believe women and girls who report being sexually assaulted or abused and to support them as they share their story with the proper legal authorities.

As we minister to those who have experienced trauma, let us remember that we do not worship a distant, unapproachable

God. Jesus understands what it is to endure trauma (Mark 15:19; Luke 23:33; John 19:1). We should all take comfort in the fact that God knows our circumstances and is with us in them. We are not alone or forgotten. The situation may seem hopeless, but he has promised to never forsake us (Deuteronomy 31:6).

THE REST OF THE STORY

It's been almost a year now since the storm, and Duncan is doing well. The family's home was so severely damaged that it is still being repaired. Duncan only sees his therapist once a month and visits the house about once a week. He is sleeping in his own room again and hasn't wet the bed in months. Jana said Duncan has almost completely recovered but still acts differently as a result of the storm. "He's always checking the weather online, particularly since hurricane season started again. Rainy days are difficult, and he also doesn't like to be away from the family for any period of time."

11

Obsessive Compulsive and Related Disorders

Probably the most heartbreaking thing as a parent is the fact that OCD has taken away much of my daughter's childhood innocence.

BRITNEY HOLDEN

LENA NEVER THOUGHT MUCH ABOUT her daughter Katy's eccentricities. Even as a young child, Katy was very concerned about germs and would often carry a bottle of cleaner and a rag around the house. She would wash her hands frequently and didn't like to touch door knobs. While some of her behaviors may have seemed odd to those outside the family, they didn't negatively affect her daily life. Katy was a straight-A student with lots of friends.

Lena thought it strange that Katy was calling her at work. When she answered the phone, Katy was hysterical, begging her mother to come home. Lena asked what was wrong, but Katy just kept begging her to come home. When Lena arrived home, Katy was weeping uncontrollably. Again, Lena asked what was wrong, and all Lena would say is, "You're going to think I'm crazy." This went on for hours as Lena held her fourteen-year-old daughter on the couch. At some point, the exhausted mother dozed off for a few minutes. When she woke up, Katy was gone. Lena found Katy kneeling in her room staring at the ceiling. "She was making strange gestures with her arms and seemed to be speaking a foreign language." Over the next few weeks things became worse. Katy's grades dropped significantly, she became withdrawn and struggled even to bath and dress. Lena spoke with a close friend who suggested that she have Katy assessed by a child psychologist.

CHARACTERISTIC SYMPTOMS

The obsessive-compulsive and related disorders are characterized by recurrent thoughts (obsessions) or rituals (compulsions) that cause severe discomfort and interfere with day-to-day functioning. Although children and adults experience many of the same obsessions and compulsions, children often express their disorder in unique ways. Unlike adults, children may not recognize that their obsessions are senseless and that their compulsions are excessive.

Obsessions are persistent thoughts or urges that one recognizes as intrusive and unwanted and that result in marked distress. Common obsessions include fear of germs or contamination, forbidden or taboo thoughts, religion, aggressive thoughts toward others or self, and placing items in a symmetrical or perfect order.

Compulsions are rituals that are performed to try to prevent or stop anxiety. For instance, a teen with this type of disorder may be obsessed with germs and dirt, constantly fearful of contamination. In an attempt to deal with his fear, he washes his hands over and over, hundreds of times throughout the day. Even when children with this condition recognize what they are doing is senseless, they are unable to stop.

DIAGNOSIS

In the seventeenth century, obsessions and compulsions were often described as symptoms of religious melancholy. Around this time, a new word for obsessions and compulsions came into usage, *scrupulosity*. In 1660, Jeremy Taylor, bishop of Down and Connor, Ireland, was referring to obsessional doubting when he wrote "[A scruple] is trouble where the trouble is over, a doubt when doubts are resolved."[1] Nowadays most people understand scrupulosity to mean obsessive religiosity, but in earlier centuries it encompassed all types of obsessions and compulsions.

By the 1700s, clergy deferred to physicians' expertise in treating obsessions and compulsions. Physicians of the 1700s and 1800s described many types of obsessions and compulsions, including compulsive washing, compulsive checking, obsessive fear of syphilis, and aggressive and sexual obsessions. The shift to a primarily medical understanding of obsessions and compulsions had serious consequences for those afflicted; the most dramatic consequence being the institutionalization of sufferers in asylums.

Nineteenth-century researchers gave many specific types of obsessions and compulsions their own names, for instance, arithmomania (compulsive counting), mysophobia (obsessive fear of contamination), and délire du toucher (touching compulsions). They also debated whether or not obsessions and compulsions should be considered a form of insanity. By the end of the century, a consensus had been reached that an obsession and compulsion was a neurosis.[2] As this consensus developed, physicians began to voice opposition to institutionalizing in asylums persons with obsessions and compulsions.

Two figures dominated the early twentieth-century history of OCD: the French neurologist Pierre Janet and the Austrian neurologist Sigmund Freud. While Janet expanded on existing medical ideas, Freud called the illness *Zwangsneurose*. In England this term was translated as "obsession," and in America it became "compulsion." The term *obsessive-compulsive* was eventually adopted as a compromise. Pierre Janet was the first to describe a pediatric case of OCD.[3]

In the 1952 DSM-I, *obsessive-compulsive reaction* was listed as a psychoneurotic disorder. In 1968 with the publication of the DSM-II, the disorder was classified as a neurosis and renamed *obsessive-compulsive neurosis*. Subsequent editions of the DSM (III, III-R, IV, IV-TR) listed *obsessive-compulsive disorder* under anxiety disorders. In the most recent edition of the manual, DSM-5, all of the obsessive-compulsive disorders are for the first time grouped together in a single category. The primary obsessive-compulsive disorders are obsessive-compulsive disorder, body dysmorphic disorder, hoarding disorder, trichotillomania, and excoriation disorder.

Obsessive-compulsive disorder (OCD) is characterized by unwanted and disturbing thoughts, images, or urges (obsessions) that cause a great deal of anxiety or discomfort that the individual tries to reduce by engaging in repetitive behaviors or mental acts (compulsions).

Body dysmorphic disorder (BDD) is characterized by obsessional thinking about one or more perceived defects or flaws in one's appearance: a flaw that to others is either minor or not observable. The child or adolescent may feel so ashamed and anxious because of the "flaw" that they avoid social situations.

Hoarding disorder is characterized by an inability to discard possessions because of a perceived need to save them. A child with hoarding disorder will experience significant distress even at the thought of getting rid of certain items. Due to the child or teen's inability to part with their possessions, an excessive accumulation of items, regardless of their actual value, is likely to occur.[4]

Trichotillomania, also called "hair-pulling disorder," is characterized by recurrent, irresistible urges to pull out hair from one's scalp, eyebrows, or other areas of the body, despite trying to stop.

Excoriation disorder, also called "dermatillomania," is characterized by repeated, compulsive picking at one's own skin, resulting in skin lesions.

After the assessment, the child psychologist diagnosed Kathy with depression and referred her to a child psychiatrist. After her own assessment of Katy, the psychiatrist felt that depression did not fully explain the young girl's problems. She referred the family to a child and adolescent psychiatric facility two hours away that could do a more detailed assessment. The results of that assessment showed that Katy was suffering from obsessive-compulsive disorder (OCD). More specifically, she was having obsessional thoughts about germs and contamination as well as troubling intrusive thoughts about cursing God and sexual sin.

PREVALENCE AND AGE OF ONSET

The prevalence and onset of obsessive-compulsive disorders are quite similar. The prevalence of OCD among children and adolescents is estimated to be 2 percent of the population. Manifestations of the disorder usually appear by age ten or earlier. Boys are more commonly affected in childhood. From adolescence onward, the prevalence in boys and girls is the same. BDD is estimated to occur in 2 percent of the population. The median age of onset for BDD is fifteen years, with males and females affected equally. Epidemiological studies suggest 2 percent of children and adolescents presents with problematic hoarding. Hoarding symptoms often first emerge in early adolescence. Lifetime prevalence of trichotillomania is estimated to be 1 percent of the population. Females are more frequently affected than males with the peak prevalence occurring between four and seventeen. Excoriation disorder occurs in 2 percent of the population. The onset of skin picking is most often in adolescence, commonly coinciding with or following the onset of puberty. Three-quarters or more of individuals with excoriation disorder are female.

RISK FACTORS

A number of factors have been shown to increase a child's risk of developing an obsessive-compulsive disorder. Prenatal and perinatal factors associated with increased risk include maternal smoking, a cesarean section delivery, preterm birth, low birth weight, large size for gestational age, breech presentation at labor, and a low Apgar scores. Negative childhood experiences such as physical or sexual abuse or other stressful or traumatic events also increase a child's risk. Children with more negative temperaments and behavioral inhibition are also more at risk to develop an obsessive-compulsive disorder as are those with first-degree relatives who have OCD.[5]

"Some parents have reported that OCD symptoms occurred almost overnight, as if a switch were flipped; their child went to bed as the child they knew and woke up a stranger."[6] This type of sudden-onset OCD is known as pediatric acute-onset neuropsychiatric syndrome (PANS). PANS results from an infection that damages the child's brain. Infections that can trigger PANS include Lyme disease, mononucleosis, the flu virus, and strep.

> The two major criteria for PANS are an abrupt and dramatic onset of OCD symptoms that is associated with significant impairment and the simultaneous, rapid onset of other symptoms from at least two of the following categories: anxiety, emotional instability and/or depression; irritability, aggression, and/or oppositional behaviors; behavioral regression; sudden deterioration in school performance; sensory or motor abnormalities, especially handwriting difficulties; and somatic, or physical signs and symptoms.[7]

NEUROBIOLOGY

Heritability. Twin and family studies have provided evidence that genetic factors are involved in the transmission and expression of obsessive-compulsive disorders. Twin studies have consistently found a higher concordance rate in identical (monozygotic) twins compared to fraternal (dizygotic) twins for the obsessive-compulsive disorders. The heritability for these disorders is estimated to be 48 percent for OCD, 43 percent for body dysmorphic disorder, 51 percent for hoarding disorder, 76 percent for trichotillomania, and 47 percent for excoriation disorder. Family studies have also shown increased rates of obsessive-compulsive disorders in the first-degree relatives of children with OCD.[8]

Neuroanatomy. Brain-imaging studies using children and adolescents diagnosed with OCD have found a number of neuroanatomical abnormalities related to the disorder, including increased gray matter density in the orbital frontal cortex, larger anterior cingulate cortex volumes, smaller striatal volumes, and increased thalamic volumes. Together these brain regions form a frontal-striatal-thalamic circuit involved in the selection and perception of important information, manipulation of information in working memory, planning and organization, behavioral control, adaptation to changes, and decision making. Children with OCD show reduced activation in this circuit compared to health controls. This neural disruption in behavioral control and adaption to change appears to influence the repetitive behaviors that characterize the illness.[9]

Neurochemistry. Several studies have found disruption in the excitatory neurotransmitter glutamate to be associated with OCD symptoms. Consistent with the neuroanatomical results previously described, glutamate concentration levels have been shown to be higher in the left caudate nucleus (part of the striatum) and lower in the anterior cingulate of pediatric OCD subjects. Increased glutamate concentrations in the caudate nucleus were found to normalize after treatment with selective serotonin reuptake inhibitors (SSRIs). This normalization of glutamate levels was associated with a reduction in OCD symptom severity. In addition, a variant in a gene that codes for the glutamate receptor is predictive of an OCD diagnosis. The results of these studies offer significant evidence for the role of altered glutamate neurotransmission in OCD.[10]

TREATMENT

The obsessive-compulsive disorders, like many psychological disorders, are most effectively treated with a combination of medication and therapy.

Behavioral therapy. Exposure and response prevention (ERP) is the best studied and most effective psychological intervention for OCD. The exposure in ERP refers to exposing the child or adolescent to the thoughts, images, objects, and situations that make them anxious or initiate obsessional thinking. The response prevention part of ERP refers to making a choice not to perform a compulsive behavior once the anxiety or obsessions have been triggered. The therapy begins under the guidance of a therapist; after repeated sessions the child learns to perform the ERP exercises on their own to help manage symptoms.[11]

Pharmacotherapy. Selective serotonin reuptake inhibitors (SSRIs) are the primary medication used in the treatment of obsessive-compulsive disorders. A number of SSRIs have received FDA approval for treating OCD in children, including fluvoxamine (Luvox; seven years and up), fluoxetine (Prozac; seven years and up), and sertraline (Zoloft; six years and up).

As mentioned in previous chapters, there is an increased risk of suicidal thinking and behavior in children and adolescents taking antidepressant medications, a risk that should be weighed against the potential benefits of the medication.

The tricyclic antidepressant clomipramine (Anafranil; ten years and up) has also been FDA-approved for treating OCD in children and adolescents. Tricyclic antidepressants affect a wider range of neurotransmitters, but because the side effects of these medications can be severe, most physicians and patients prefer the SSRIs.

Soon after the OCD diagnosis, Katy began weekly therapy and was prescribed medication. Lena said that the medication was very helpful. "Katy's functioning improved and her grades came back up." Katy continued therapy and medication throughout her sophomore and junior years of high school. Because she had not shown any significant symptoms for more than a year, the psychiatrist decided to wean Katy off medication the summer before her senior year. Lena said, "At first she was fine, but as the stress of school built up, her symptoms started to reappear." The psychiatrist quickly started the medication again. While this did bring some improvement, she was not as good as she had been before she had stopped the medication. Katy was able to successfully complete high school and graduated later that year.

Given how quickly Katy's OCD symptoms had returned without the medication, her psychiatrist recommended she enroll in a six-week intensive outpatient treatment program that specialized in exposure and response prevention (ERP). In this program Katy worked with therapists and counselors eight hours a day, four days a week. Lena said that the program "was a miracle." Katy, now eighteen, was better than she had ever been. It was decided that Katy should continue on medication for another year and find a therapist in her hometown trained in ERP therapy. Katy began taking classes at the local junior college that fall. Lena said that because they live in a small town, it was impossible to find a local therapist trained in ERP. "Since we couldn't find a therapist, I started working with her at home. Parents attended all the sessions in the intensive outpatient program, and they had trained us how to work with our kids." A little over a year later, Katy was weaned off her medication.

A BIBLICAL PERSPECTIVE

While reports of individuals displaying OCD symptoms have survived from biblical times, no example of the disorder appears in the Scriptures.[12] The Bible does, however, offer insights into one of the primary symptoms of the obsessive-compulsive disorders: distressing, intrusive, and unwanted thoughts.

Psalm 139 is a wonderful comfort for those caring for a child with an obsessive-compulsive disorder.

> You have searched me, LORD,
>   and you know me.
> You know when I sit and when I rise;
>   you perceive my thoughts from afar.

> You discern my going out and my lying down;
> you are familiar with all my ways.
> Before a word is on my tongue
> you, Lord, know it completely. (Psalm 139:1-4 NIV)

God knows each child intimately, every thought, every action. He can separate their intrusive thoughts and compulsive behaviors from those they control. He is not surprised or put off by their odd thoughts and behaviors. The child is not simply a diagnosis to him but is his beloved child.

> You hem me in behind and before,
> and you lay your hand upon me.
> Such knowledge is too wonderful for me,
> too lofty for me to attain.
> Where can I go from your Spirit?
> Where can I flee from your presence?
> If I go up to the heavens, you are there;
> if I make my bed in the depths, you are there.
> If I rise on the wings of the dawn,
> if I settle on the far side of the sea,
> even there your hand will guide me,
> your right hand will hold me fast.
> If I say, "Surely the darkness will hide me
> and the light become night around me,"
> even the darkness will not be dark to you;
> the night will shine like the day,
> for darkness is as light to you. (Psalm 139:5-12 NIV)

He is present with all children at all times, even when the illness is at its worst. He is there to guide, to support, and to comfort children and their parents. Remind the child that God's presence is a constant and stable anchor in the chaos of mental illness.

For you created my inmost being;
  you knit me together in my mother's womb.
I praise you because I am fearfully and wonderfully made;
  your works are wonderful,
  I know that full well.
My frame was not hidden from you
  when I was made in the secret place,
  when I was woven together in the depths of the earth.
Your eyes saw my unformed body;
  all the days ordained for me were written in your book
  before one of them came to be.
    (Psalm 139:13-16 NIV)

While a child's body and mind may have been damaged by our fallen world, they are not a divine mistake. Their creation was the will of God. He has instilled in the child talents and gifts that we have the opportunity to actively nurture and help them develop.

How precious to me are your thoughts, God!
  How vast is the sum of them!
Were I to count them,
  they would outnumber the grains of sand—

when I awake, I am still with you.
(Psalm 139:17-18 NIV)

God is good and his plans for all children are good too. A mental disorder in no way limits or hinders the plans God has ordained for them. Look beyond the illness and see their potential through God's eyes. His loving thoughts for a child outnumber the grains of sand on the beach.

Search me, God, and know my heart;
test me and know my anxious thoughts.
See if there is any offensive way in me,
and lead me in the way everlasting.
(Psalm 139:23-24 NIV)

God not only knows a child's thoughts but also their heart. While he celebrates children's joys, he also feels their pain and frustration. Psalm 139 ends with perhaps the greatest promise of all, an opportunity to be "led in the way everlasting": to know God and enjoy his presence forever. God is pursuing a relationship with a child even in the mess that is mental illness.

Children—with all their odd thoughts and behaviors—are created by a loving, sovereign God. God doesn't make mistakes. He knew each child before their birth. He formed them in the womb and brought them into the world. God has given children to us as a gift, a reward. A child is no less of a gift because they have OCD. Neither is a child any less loved by God. While we may struggle to understand such a child, God knows their every thought. He chose their parents and has equipped them, as believers in Christ, with all the love and patience necessary to raise their child. Do not allow the world to define a child. See each child for who they are, a beloved child of God, made in his image.

THE REST OF THE STORY

Recently, Katy completed her associate's degree at the junior college and is preparing to move out of state to continue her education. Lena said, "Katy is doing very well. She still checks in with her psychiatrist occasionally but isn't taking any medication. I still almost daily help her practice the skills she learned in therapy. We have found that the more she talks about her intrusive thoughts the better."

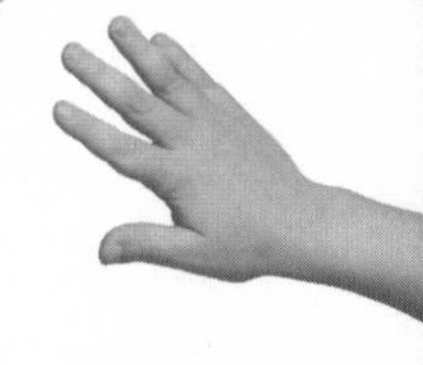

12

Worthless

Eating Disorders

How could my child be dying in front of me?
I knew I had to do something, but I
did not know where to begin.

PEGGY CLAUDE-PIERRE

PRIOR TO THE NINTH GRADE, Mina had always done well in school. In fact her mother, Carla, described her as perfectionistic when it came to grades. But in high school Mina began to struggle with severe anxiety. As a result, good grades became hard to obtain, and it was difficult for Mina to maintain friendships. Her one place of peace was performing on the stage. Mina had been in dance and theater classes from an early age, and as a freshman she was active in drama. Things changed radically for the family during Mina's sophomore year. Mina's father abandoned the family and subsequently divorced her mother. Due to changes in their finances, Mina had to drop out of the private academy she had attended since kindergarten and transfer to public school. While the midyear move was difficult, she was accepted to the district's school for the performing arts so she could continue to pursue her first love.

Not long after starting at her new school Mina was told by the dance program director "to lose weight" even though she was athletic and fit. Carla was upset when she found out and met with the school's principal to voice her disapproval. The principal minimized the issue and nothing was done. Later that same year, Carla received a frightening phone call from the school informing her that Mina had a seizure. The distraught mother rushed to the school and took her daughter to the emergency room. Tests at the hospital showed nothing, and no reason was ever found for the seizure. "The signs were there, but I missed them," Carla said. "During her junior year, I noticed her hair was thinning, so we went to the doctor. He found she had slight hypothyroidism, and I assumed that was the reason for the hair loss. I didn't realize that the seizure and hair loss were the signs of a developing binge-eating disorder."

CHARACTERISTIC SYMPTOMS

Eating disorders are characterized by an unhealthy preoccupation with weight, body shape, and food, leading to dangerous eating behaviors. Many adolescents with an eating disorder do not realize they have a problem, or if they do they go to extraordinary lengths to hide the signs of their disorder. A teen with an eating disorder may appear healthy yet be extremely ill. This was the case with Mina. She appeared physically well and worked hard to hide her disordered eating.

An *unhealthy preoccupation* with body shape and weight can manifest behaviorally in a variety of ways, including extreme dieting, weighing oneself multiple times a day, obsessive calorie counting, hoarding or hiding food, body checking (e.g., compulsively looking in the mirror), food rituals (e.g., excessive chewing), refusal to eat certain foods, progressing to restrictions against whole categories of food (e.g., no carbohydrates), skipping meals or taking small portions of food at regular meals, and excessive exercising. Engaging in any of these behaviors can be a slippery slope for many teens because the shift from normal eating to disordered eating to eating disorder happens more quickly than expected.

DIAGNOSIS

While cultural pressures have clearly played a role in the frequency of eating disorders, written accounts of the disorders have existed since the seventeenth century, long before celebrity diets, supermodels, and television commercials.

In 1689, Richard Morton, an English physician, published the first medical account of anorexia, what he called "nervous consumption," in a text titled *A Treatise of Consumption*. A number of case reports of the disorder appeared throughout the eighteenth and early nineteenth centuries, but Dr. Charles Lasègue, a French physician, first used the term *anorexia* to describe the disorder in a set of papers published in 1873. French neurologist Pierre Janet first described patients with bulimic behaviors in 1903, but it was not until 1979 that British psychiatrist Gerald Russell published the first formal medical paper on bulimia nervosa.[1] Binge-eating disorder was first described in 1959 by American psychiatrist Albert Stunkard, who called it "night eating syndrome."[2] Presently the DSM-5 includes three primary eating disorder diagnoses: anorexia nervosa, bulimia nervosa, and binge-eating disorder.

Anorexia nervosa is characterized by a body weight that is significantly less than that minimally expected for age and height. This dangerously low body weight is usually maintained by dieting, fasting, or excessive exercise. There are two specific subtypes of the disorder: *restricting type* and *binge-eating/purging type*. Individuals with the restricting subtype do not regularly engage in binge eating or purging behavior, while those with the binge-eating/purging subtype do. Binge eating is an impulsive consumption of an excessively large amount of food over a relatively short period of time. Purging behaviors include self-induced vomiting and the abuse of laxatives, diuretics (water pills), or enemas in an attempt to prevent weight gain.

Bulimia nervosa is characterized by regular episodes of binge eating followed by inappropriate compensatory behaviors meant to prevent weight gain. These compensatory behaviors include purging, the misuse of weight-loss medications, fasting, and excessive exercise. For a diagnosis of bulimia nervosa, the binge eating and compensatory behaviors must have occurred at least twice a week for at least three months. Individuals with bulimia are usually normal weight, but they can be slightly underweight or overweight.

Binge-eating disorder is characterized by recurrent episodes of binge eating; feelings of a loss of control during the binge; shame, distress, or guilt afterward; and regularly using unhealthy compensatory measures (e.g., purging) to counter the binge eating. Individuals with binge-eating disorder are usually overweight, although the disorder is distinct from obesity.

During her junior year, Mina's hidden binge-eating disorder became too much, and she asked her mother if she could finish high school online. Carla felt that Mina's problems were primarily related to the divorce and sought a therapist for her. Mina successfully completed high school online and was awarded a full scholarship to a prestigious performing arts college in New York.

The transition to living in New York was difficult for Mina. She was depressed, anxious, and hiding a serious binge-eating disorder. Carla said that when Mina came home for the semester break, she noticed that her always athletic and fit daughter was now out of shape and slightly overweight. By the end of her freshman year, Mina asked her mother if she could "take some time off from college to get herself together." Carla agreed, so Mina found a job at a local sweets shop and moved back in with her mother and stepfather.

Carla reported that several months later they started to have a pest problem in the house. "No matter how much I cleaned and sprayed there were more and more bugs." Mina lived in a separate part of the house with her own bathroom. Carla said, "Since she was older and in college, we tried to let her have her own space. She was responsible for cleaning her room and bathroom." Due to the pest infestation, Carla decided to clean in Mina's room as well. "When I opened the door, I couldn't believe what I saw. There were crumbs and food wrappers everywhere. Half-eaten food was lying out on the dresser and her closet was full of bags of cookies and chocolates. As soon as Mina got home, I confronted her." She admitted that she had been struggling with binge eating for some time. She was bringing home the leftover cookies and candies from the sweets shop each day and hiding them in her closet. At night she would binge eat, consuming as many as five thousand calories in a single binge.

PREVALENCE AND AGE OF ONSET

The estimated lifetime prevalence rates for eating disorders in adolescents are as follows: anorexia nervosa (0.3 percent), bulimia nervosa (0.9 percent), and binge-eating disorder (1.6 percent). Eating disorders are ten times more prevalent among girls as boys. The peak age of onset is between fourteen and eighteen years old, with few cases occurring before puberty.[3] The onset of these disorders is often associated with a stressful life event or trauma. Anorexia nervosa has the highest fatality rate of any mental disorder. It is estimated that 4 percent of anorexic individuals die from complications of the disease. Adolescents with bulimia nervosa show significantly high rates of self-harm and suicidality.[4]

RISK FACTORS

A number of factors have been shown to increase an adolescent's risk of developing an eating disorder. Prenatal and perinatal risk factors include maternal smoking, prematurity, and low birth weight. Psychological risk factors include negative self-evaluation, heightened perfectionism, low self-esteem, body dissatisfaction, childhood anxiety disorder or obsessional traits, depressive symptoms, and feelings of inadequacy. Environmental factors that have been shown to influence the development of eating disorders consist of a maternal focus on weight and appearance issues, family conflict, childhood physical or sexual abuse, an achievement-oriented family, and a culture that emphasizes thinness and places a high value on obtaining the "perfect body."[5] A number of these factors were present in Mina's life, resulting in significant psychological distress. Her heightened perfectionism, family conflict leading to divorce, financial problems, school changes, and a dance teacher critical of her weight all contributed to the manifestation of her binge-eating disorder.

NEUROBIOLOGY

Heritability. Family and twin studies have consistently demonstrated that genetic factors play a part in the expression of eating disorders. Family studies have found significantly greater lifetime prevalence rates for eating disorders in the first-degree relatives of adolescents with eating disorders. Similarly, twin studies have shown a higher concordance rate in identical (monozygotic) twins with eating disorders compared to fraternal (dizygotic) twins. The heritability for these disorders is estimated to be 58 percent for anorexia nervosa, 59 percent for bulimia nervosa, and 57 percent for binge-eating disorder.[6]

Neuroanatomy. Studies have shown the hypothalamic-pituitary-adrenal axis (HPA) to be involved in the development of eating disorders. The HPA is part of the endocrine system and is made up of the hypothalamus (a structure on the lower aspect of the brain), the pituitary gland (a small pea-shaped gland below the hypothalamus, in the middle of the head), and the adrenal glands (located on top of the kidneys). The HPA is involved in controlling our reaction to stress and regulating appetite, weight, digestion, mood, and immune system response. Studies suggest that a dysfunction in the HPA, most likely brought about by a combination of negative early life experiences (e.g., sexual abuse) and genetic factors, leaves the adolescent female vulnerable to chronic stress. This vulnerability is intensified by the hormonal changes that occur at puberty (which takes place just prior to the most common age of onset for the eating disorders). Studies suggest that exposure to a significant stressor during this period results in a dysregulated HPA response, leading to a chronic reduction in appetite and weight.[7]

Neurochemistry. The neurotransmitter most often thought to be related to eating disorders is serotonin (5-HT). Research has shown that an increase in the activity of the brain's serotonergic system leads to a reduction in appetite. And indeed, several studies with anorexic patients have found increased activity in this neurotransmitter system. In addition, research shows that increased serotonergic activity is related to many of the characteristics commonly seen in adolescents with anorexia nervosa, such as behavioral inhibition, anxiety, and obsessive-compulsive tendencies. Some researchers hypothesize that starvation actually makes adolescents with anorexia feel better by decreasing the 5-HT in their brains.[8]

Adolescents with bulimia nervosa and binge-eating disorder appear to have a somewhat different alteration in the 5-HT system than those with anorexia. Research suggests that adolescents with bulimia nervosa and binge-eating disorder suffer from chronically low 5-HT levels, which is thought to contribute to binge eating in an attempt to relieve the depressed mood caused by this low serotonin. Low levels of 5-HT have been shown to be related to many of the characteristics commonly seen in adolescents with bulimia nervosa and binge-eating disorder, such as impulsivity, irritability, and self-harm.[9]

TREATMENT

Eating disorders can be effectively treated, and early diagnosis and intervention significantly increase the chances of a positive outcome. As with all mental disorders, a comprehensive initial assessment is the first step in effectively treating the problem. This assessment will determine the medical, nutritional, and psychological status of the adolescent and give the treatment team the information necessary to begin an appropriate intervention.

Hospitalization. For medically unstable adolescents with anorexia nervosa, the acute management of severe weight loss is the top priority. This treatment is normally done in an inpatient hospital setting. Problems related to malnutrition are the focus in this phase of treatment, and in many cases intravenous or tube feeding are recommended to restore weight. In addition to medical care and monitoring, the patient also receives nutritional counseling and the initial stages of therapy in this setting.

Psychosocial treatment. The primary therapeutic treatment used in anorexia nervosa is Maudsley family therapy, also called family-based treatment (FBT). FBT "is based on the idea that families make accommodations in feeding their child that initially appear useful in combating anorexia, but these ultimately become maladaptive, disrupting both the development of the adolescent and perpetuating the behaviors that maintain the disorder.

Treatment aims to identify and help the family modify these accommodations."[10] The most effective therapeutic approach for bulimia nervosa and binge-eating disorder is cognitive-behavioral therapy (CBT). In CBT, the focus is on helping the adolescent gain control of unhealthy eating behaviors and altering their distorted (deceptive) thinking (e.g., body dissatisfaction).[11]

Pharmacotherapy. Presently, only two medications have been approved by the FDA for the treatment of eating disorders: fluoxetine (Prozac) for bulimia nervosa and lisdexamfetamine (Vyvanse) for binge-eating disorder. Prozac is a selective serotonin reuptake inhibitor (SSRI), while Vyvanse is a psychostimulant more commonly prescribed for ADHD. No medication has yet been FDA-approved for the treatment of anorexia nervosa.

Research has shown that SSRIs can be effective in treating eating disorders. Individuals with anorexia nervosa do not respond well to the SSRIs when they are malnourished and underweight. Once a normal weight and diet have been established, however, the SSRIs can help to maintain long-term remission of symptoms and prevent relapse. SSRIs are often used in the initial phases of treating individuals with bulimia nervosa and binge-eating disorder for problems related to mood and impulse control. In adolescents with binge-eating disorder who do not respond to treatment with an SSRI, the antiepileptic medication topiramate (Topamax) or lisdexamfetamine (Vyvanse) are often prescribed.

Carla and Mina considered inpatient treatment but decided to try outpatient care first. Mina found a psychiatrist who prescribed her medication, and she began weekly therapy. The medication had little effect. Mina tried a number of medications over the next year with little benefit. Ultimately, she was taken off all medication but continued her weekly therapy. About this same time, Mina was scheduled for surgery because gastroesophageal reflux caused by binge eating had seriously damaged her esophagus.[12]

A BIBLICAL PERSPECTIVE

The biblical authors were keenly aware that emotional distress could affect an individual's eating. Multiple descriptions of individuals restricting their food intake as a result of emotional distress appear in the Scriptures; these include Hannah (1 Samuel 1:7), Jonathan (1 Samuel 20:34), King Saul (1 Samuel 28:20), King Ahab (1 Kings 21:4), Ezra (Ezra 10:6) and Paul (Acts 9:9). None of these reports, however, appear to represent disordered eating due to the short duration (a few days or less) of the food restrictions. A description of a young woman with a longer period of food restriction following a significantly distressing event appears in the deuterocanonical book of Judith.

The book of Judith was written in the first century BC and describes events occurring during an Assyrian invasion of Israel. The main character of the book is Judith, a young woman who lived in the city of Bethulia. Due to a number of historical inaccuracies in the text, the book of Judith is best understood as a religious historical novel.

Judith is described as a beautiful young widow in mourning. Her husband, Manasseh, died from a heat stroke during the barley harvest three years prior to the events of the book. Since his death, Judith isolated herself in a tent on the roof of her home, wore sack cloth for mourning, and restricted her food intake to two days a week and during the Jewish festivals. The length of Judith's restrictive eating (three years and four months) would have left her significantly underweight.[13]

During the invasion, the Assyrian general Holofernes and his army lay siege to Bethulia and cut off the city's water supply. After thirty-four days under siege, the text tells us that the people of Bethulia were in misery and begged the leaders of the town to surrender. Judith is angered by their willingness to surrender and confronts the leaders of the town. She reminds them of God's faithfulness to Israel in the past and tells them that God will deliver Israel from the Assyrians by her hand as proof of his faithfulness.

Judith prays for God to use her against the Assyrians. She then bathes, puts on perfume, dresses provocatively, and adorns herself with jewelry. That night she and her maid leave the city and are quickly captured by an Assyrian patrol. They are taken to the Assyrian camp and brought before Holofernes. Judith lies to the general, telling him that she has information that will help him take the city without the loss of a single soldier. Holofernes is captivated by Judith's beauty and allows her to stay in the camp. One evening Judith is invited to Holofernes's tent for a banquet. Once they are left alone, Judith takes advantage of the general's intoxication and decapitates him with his own sword. She returns to Bethulia with his head as a trophy. Judith's actions embolden the Israelites to rout the Assyrians and stop the invasion.

Within eating disorders, we clearly see how environmental factors (e.g., a stressful event or trauma) can interact with a physical vulnerability (e.g., HPA dysregulation, overactive or underactive serotonin system), mental distortions (e.g., negative self-image), and spiritual deception (e.g., one's worth is based on physical appearance) to result in the symptoms of a mental illness (e.g., purging, self-starvation). Eating disorders aren't really about food but rather about how individuals view themselves and the world around them.

In Judith's case, the sudden death of her husband left her heartbroken and alone. Her grief at the loss of Manasseh led to a deep, long-lasting depression that distorted the spiritual discipline of fasting into a compulsive, unhealthy approach to eating. In a world that seemed totally out of control, Judith took control of the only thing she could, when and what she ate. Despite her struggles, Judith led a life devoted to God, and the people of Bethulia admired her for her piety (Judith 8:8).

The story of Judith reminds us that disordered eating is not the result of some spiritual weakness but rather the result of a complex interaction between the environment and biology.

Despite her struggles, Judith was pursuing God, and in a dark time he used her to rescue his people. Encourage your children that God designed them as they are knit together before the very foundation of time (Psalm 139). God is pleased with them. They are valued, loved, and royal, held in high esteem by the Creator of the universe (1 Peter 2:9).

THE REST OF THE STORY

It took a year of weekly therapy before Mina's eating disorder was under control. After that, she returned to college and gradually began taking classes again. Mina successfully graduated from college and today works for a nonprofit organization in New York. While her binge-eating disorder has been under control for several years, she still struggles with depression and still regularly sees a therapist.

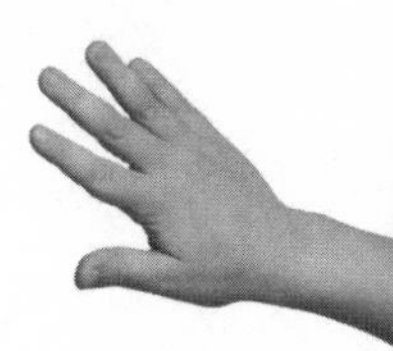

13

Being Holistic

You shall love the Lord your God with all your heart, and with all your soul, and with all your strength, and with all your mind; and your neighbor as yourself.

LUKE 10:27

GOD HAS CREATED ALL CHILDREN as the union of a physical body with an immaterial mind and spirit. Because of this, when a child struggles with a mental disorder, they require a holistic approach to care that takes into account all aspects of their being: physical, mental, spiritual, and relational. A holistic approach to mental-health care relieves physical and psychological suffering while revealing the unconditional love and limitless grace only available through a personal relationship with Jesus.

While it is understood that each family will have unique challenges and issues related to their child's specific disorder, the physical, mental, spiritual, and relational needs listed are general principles that have been found to be helpful for most mental-health difficulties. Take your time and don't feel like you have to rush to get everything in place all at once. Everyone is different, so be patient and keep learning what does and doesn't work for the child. As a child heals, they will be able to do more and will move beyond a highly structured daily routine or schedule. Adjust accordingly as the child becomes more independent and successful at navigating daily life.

PHYSICAL NEEDS

The physical needs associated with a mental disorder go far beyond simply taking medication; it also includes sleep, nutrition, and regular physical activity. Keeping the body (and brain) healthy will help lessen the severity of symptoms related to the disorder and can enhance the action of the medication.

Sleeping well. Sleep problems affect the vast majority of children and adolescents living with mental-health difficulties, compared to only 10-18 percent of the general population.[1] The two most common sleep-related complaints in children diagnosed with a mental disorder are (1) not being able to fall asleep (onset insomnia), and (2) waking up early and not being able to go back to sleep (late insomnia). Sleep deprivation can trigger symptoms such as suicidal thoughts, paranoia, agitation, and hyperactivity. Activities that can increase restfulness include having a set bedtime and routine, having a set wake-up time, lowering the bedroom's temperature at night, regular physical activity, reducing the use of caffeine, avoiding video screens for an hour before bedtime, and talking with the child's psychiatrist about the effects of his medication on sleep.

Pharmacotherapy. The primary function of medication is to alter the way nerve cells (neurons) in the brain function. This is done by changing the number of chemical messengers (called neurotransmitter) the nerve cells release or by changing the electrical properties of the nerve cell's membrane.

Every child responds to medication differently, and it is normal to try many different medications until the best one is found for a child. Educate yourself about the medications that have been prescribed (suggested sources of information: psychiatrist, pharmacist, WebMD, drug company website, mentalhealthgateway.org). Know what they do, how they work, their potential side effects, interactions with food and other medications, and how sensitive the effects of the drug are to missed doses or noncompliance. Many psychiatric medications are deadly if used in an overdose. For this reason, medication should be stored in a place not accessible to the child. Organize the medications in such a way that they can be taken accurately and with ease (e.g., daily pill-dispensing boxes).

Learning to relax. The physical symptoms of stress and anxiety (heart racing, sweating, shortness of breath, nausea) can be overwhelming. Relaxation techniques such as focused breathing, progressive muscle relaxation, meditation, coloring, and listening to music can be helpful during these episodes of panic but can also help when done on a daily basis to bring down a child's general level of stress. If one relaxation technique doesn't work for a child, have them try another, everyone is different.

Eating healthy. A balanced and nutritious diet promotes brain health and stabilizes mood. In addition, a healthy diet combats weight gain, a common side effect of psychiatric medication. In contrast, junk food and foods high in sugar increase weight gain, deplete energy levels, and limit a child's ability to concentrate for extended periods of time. A diet that includes fruits, vegetables, whole grains, healthy fats (e.g., avocado, olive oil, coconut oil), lean meats, poultry, fish, beans, eggs, and nuts (much like the Paleo or Whole Food Plan) replenishes electrolytes and amino acids. This in turns affects neurotransmitters in the brain and can enhance the effects of medication. In some cases, nutritional supplements, such as essential fatty acids, may be helpful. These supplements should be used in addition to but not in place of psychiatric medication. Always check with the doctor before giving a nutritional supplement to a child to be sure that it will not negatively interact with prescribed medications.

Regular physical activity. Being physically active is just as important to a child's mental health as eating right. Children need sixty minutes of moderate to vigorous active play every day. This does not need to be an intense structured workout period but rather something fun that gets them moving and is easy to maintain (e.g., riding a bike, playing catch, walking the dog). The goal is to be regularly active in order to strengthen the body and to relieve anxiety and depressive symptoms. Regular exercise also offsets common troublesome medication side effects such as constipation, drowsiness, weight gain, fatigue, and irritability.

MENTAL NEEDS

Mental disorders are often a battle between reality and wrong or negative thoughts that overwhelm a child's mind. A structured approach to psychological needs is just as important as physical needs and includes regular therapy, healthy thinking, positive coping skills, and enjoyable mental activities.

Psychosocial treatment. Therapy is done by a licensed therapist or child psychologist and focuses on managing symptoms related to the disorder and improving a child's general quality of life. Be sure the child's therapist is using a therapeutic intervention shown to be effective in treating the child's particular disorder.

Healthy thinking. Our emotions and behaviors are the result of what we think or believe about ourselves, other people, and the world (thinking →feelings →behavior). Our thoughts shape how we interpret and evaluate what happens to us, influence our feelings about it, and provide a framework for how we should respond. Unfortunately, sometimes our interpretations, evaluations, underlying beliefs, and thoughts contain distortions, errors, and biases.

Unhealthy thinking often develops in childhood as the result of difficult life experiences (e.g., trauma) or being taught maladaptive thinking by parents and friends. We also become more prone to unhealthy thinking when we are under stress. When we are under pressure, we are more likely to take thinking shortcuts, which result in less accurate and more extreme interpretations and reactions. Our emotions are the result of what we think or believe about other people, the world, and ourselves. The more a child's thinking is characterized by distortions, the more likely the child is to experience negative emotions and engage in maladaptive behaviors.[2]

Healthy thinking does not mean positive thinking, which is only seeing the world through rose-colored glasses. No one can look at things positively all the time. Sometimes bad things happen. Healthy thinking means looking at life and the world in a balanced and accurate way.

When a child is struggling as the result of external stressors or negative symptoms, help them assess their thinking. First, determine if they have fallen into a thinking trap. Thinking traps result in less accurate interpretations of events and more extreme reactions. The following are common thinking traps that distort a child's perception of self, others, and events.

All-or-none thinking looks at things in absolute, black-and-white categories instead of on a continuum.

Overgeneralization involves thinking that a negative situation is part of a cycle of bad things that happen.

A mental filter is used to focus only on the negative part(s) of a situation and ignoring anything positive or good.

Fortune-telling is predicting that things will turn out badly without any evidence.

Emotional reasoning assumes that one's negative feelings necessarily reflect the way things really are.

Labeling (name-calling) is saying or thinking only negative things about yourself or others.

A should statement tells yourself that you or others "should" or "must" act in a certain way.

Mind reading concludes what others are thinking without any evidence or making any effort to check it out.

Personalization and blaming is believing that everything others do or say is your fault or a direct, personal reaction to you in some way.

Once we determine the thinking trap they have fallen into, we want to challenge their distorted thinking by helping them find evidence against their inaccurate thoughts. Ask them, How would God respond to your thoughts? What does the Bible say? Would you agree with those thoughts if your friend or sibling were having them? Help them form more accurate thoughts based on the new evidence. Finish by asking them how the new thoughts have changed how they feel.

Coping skills. Coping mechanisms are learned patterns of behavior used to cope. We learn from others as well as from our own experiences how to deal with stress. Negative coping choices reduce immediate feelings of stress but with time create their own problems and are best avoided (e.g., substance abuse). On the other hand, positive coping choices produce a long-term reduction in stress and enhance the overall quality of one's life.

We can actively confront a problem by gathering information, building resiliency, or changing a situation in order to adapt. A more passive coping approach is to regulate our emotional response to a challenge by suppressing negative thinking, distracting our thoughts, or learning to accept a negative situation.

When children and adolescents struggling with mental-health difficulties take direct positive action to cope with their disorder, they put themselves in a position of power. Active positive coping is empowering and takes away feelings of helplessness. Examples of this type of coping include asking for help, talking with friends, problem solving, setting goals, exercising, taking time out when they need a break, and praying.

Recognizing cycles and triggers. A recovery-orientated lifestyle requires understanding and being educated about the predictable cycles and triggers of negative symptoms in order to better manage them. During times of stability, common signs often appear that reveal a more difficult cycle (episode) is coming (e.g., oversleeping, increasing irritability, not eating, academic problems, increasing anxiety). Negative cycles triggered by seasonal changes, events, or transitional times (e.g., holidays, end of the school semester) can be predicted and minimized. Without a plan or process to help minimize these cycles or triggers, life will be driven by the child's symptoms. Taking a preventative, proactive approach when these signs appear will assist in helping the child maintain greater stability and health.

Engaging the mind. Cognitive (neural) reserve is the complexity and overlap of neural networks in the brain that provide a buffer against loss of function following aging, brain injury, or mental illness. This reserve is affected by a multitude of factors, including genes, environment, education, physical health, lifestyle, and mental activities. Evidence suggests that mental activities have a healing and protective effect on mental well-being. They provide a means of self-expression and reduce blood pressure while boosting the immune system and reducing stress. In other words, cognitive (neural) reserve can be built up. The negative symptoms associated with mental-health difficulties often cause a child or adolescent to become sedentary and isolated, resulting in a lack of mental activities and increased negative symptoms.

Within a recovery-oriented lifestyle the brain should be viewed as a muscle that requires exercise and activity to function at its best. Mental activities may be done individually or in a group setting and include painting, drawing, reading, photography, music, gardening, word games or puzzles, or other hobbies. Mental activities are just that, active! Help the child or teen avoid passive, mindless activities such as watching TV or playing video games. An hour or so of TV or video games a day is fine. We need to be concerned about excessive, mindless activities that promote isolation and minimize interactions with family and friends. In place of TV and video games, schedule a variety of physical or mental activities throughout the week.

SPIRITUAL NEEDS

The church has a significant role to play in the lives of children (and their families) struggling with mental illness. Studies have shown that religious support offers benefits to psychologically distressed children that are unavailable from general social support.[3] These benefits include a sense of value and purpose, forgiveness, and connection to a healing community. Religious support is vital to recovery and wholeness. More importantly, we serve a God who loves us deeply, who hears our desperate cries, and responds with sustaining mercy and grace.

Hope. Hope is believing the promise of better things to come despite challenges. It is not simply wishing that something bad or negative would somehow change. Hope is positively associated with perceived ability and self-worth, and negatively associated with the symptoms of depression. Hope energizes people and gives them strength to endure in a way that nothing else does. "People without hope become defeated, broken, and unable to cope with adversity. Hopeless people give up."[4]

"Christian hope is a confidence that something will come to pass because God has promised it will come to pass."[5]

Faith and hope are overlapping realities: hope is faith in the future tense. Hebrews 11:1 says, "Faith is confidence in what we hope for and assurance about what we do not see" (NIV). We must be careful to not allow circumstances to break down our hope. Circumstances change; God does not. Christian hope comes from the promises of God rooted in the work of Christ. The Scriptures were written to encourage us and to give us hope. Use God's Word to rebuild a child's hope.

Show them that heroes of faith like Elijah (1 Kings 19:4), David (Psalm 13), and Jeremiah (Lamentations 3) struggled with times of intense hopelessness. Remind them that while deep despair and hopelessness can occur in believers, God is faithful. Demonstrate to them how focusing on that single truth brought hope to the prophet Jeremiah at his lowest point:

> This I recall to my mind,
> Therefore I have hope.
> The LORD's lovingkindnesses indeed never cease,
> For His compassions never fail.
> *They* are new every morning
> great is Your faithfulness. (Lamentations 3:21-23)

Use the Scriptures to make clear that as children of the living God our hope is built on Christ (e.g., Romans 5:1-5; Colossians 1:27; 1 Timothy 1:1; Hebrews 6:17-20), who chose us, saved us, sealed us with the Holy Spirit, and promised to return and take us home.

Identity. A child's identity is not their diagnosis or mental-health difficulty! Their true identity, who they really are, is based on their value to God. Circumstances and struggles do not define them, God does. One of the common difficulties for children and adolescents living with mental illness is a disconnection or loss of emotional control. It is common for them to feel unable to connect emotionally in important relationships or even with God.

Because faith is not tangible like bodily sensations, children living with mental illness may feel condemnation or that their faith is not strong enough. They may begin to think that God does not care for them or is distant and silent. They may even question their salvation! Feeling disconnected from God can be frustrating and common, but it is not a reflection of our access to God. As his children, God has given us access to himself through prayer in all circumstances, both good and bad. He wants us to share with him our feelings, our thankfulness, and our requests for what we need. The Bible says he "longs to be gracious to you" (Isaiah 30:18). We must continually remind children of this truth so they will have a strong foundation on which to recover.

Growing spiritually. The Scriptures call us to "grow in the grace and knowledge of our Lord and Savior Jesus Christ" (2 Peter 3:18). Grace is unmerited love freely given. You don't have to be perfect to receive God's grace, only willing. Receiving God's grace is the first step in the process of spiritual growth. God knows every child afflicted with a mental illness in a deep and intimate way. His heart is to bless them and bring peace to their souls.

For children and adolescents living with mental-health difficulties, brief daily scriptural encouragements can be helpful. The focus of these encouragements should be on God's character and the child's identity and approval in Christ, not references that imply what a child must do to get better. Meditating on a single verse of Scripture or verse in a worship song is often better than a long, detailed Bible study or devotional. Tape encouraging verses on the child's mirror or write them on the mirror with a dry erase marker. Put a note in the child's lunch box with a promise from God. Studying Scripture should be a time for them to be loved by God, not a time to fight their disorder (which they cannot cure on their own). Worship is a time to come into the presence of God in a physical sense. It should not be a time of mental condemnation and overwhelming physical stimulation for the child.

Living in community. An active and supportive faith community cultivates life; isolation brings frustration and fatigue. God has called us to "rejoice with those who rejoice, and weep with those who weep" (Romans 12:15). A strong faith community offers comfort and support, gains wisdom as it learns from one another, shares and upholds common values, strengthens each other, takes risks together, and always looks to encourage one another. Many times, because of certain cycles or difficult symptoms, staying consistent with faith community events can be difficult for the families of children and adolescents living with mental illness. Others may not understand this inconsistency and back away. The key is staying connected to a few trusted and supportive people, not trying to keep up with the gathering or events that can wear one down. Living in community is more about being connected to life-giving relationships than trying to attend events with people we don't really know.

RELATIONAL NEEDS

Mental illness affects more than just the child with the disorder; it affects their entire family. Difficulties, stigma, and shame often isolate whole families trying to care for a mentally ill child from the world around them. In addition, high levels of stress and difficult symptoms can result in relational conflict requiring forgiveness and reconciliation.

Family and friends. The symptoms of mental disorders can interfere with trust, emotional closeness, communication, and effective problem solving. At the beginning of symptoms, family members and friends often look for answers or reasons for the problems other than mental illness, hoping that the symptoms are caused by some other physical problems, spiritual issues, or external stressors that can be easily removed. It is imperative that the family and friends of a child or adolescent living with mental illness gain understanding about the disorder and receive support from others. Without information to help families learn to cope with mental-health difficulties, they can lose hope and withdraw. Supportive family and friends are an important part of recovery. They can be there to listen and to help during the rough times. If people offer help, let them help. Do you need a meal, a grocery pickup, a load of laundry washed, and the like? Share specific prayer requests with trusted friends. Do not walk this road alone. A loving community provides hope!

Resolving conflict. Every relationship will have some conflict; therefore, it's important to learn and grow from them. Resolving conflicts is more about compromising to create a healthy conclusion rather than proving a point. If you push a child to embrace your point of view, it creates more tension and can come across as manipulative. If you find yourself in conflict with a child or adolescent, ask yourself if the disorder may be clouding their judgment. If so, allow yourself (and them) to take a break and return later to follow-up with more appropriate perspective and emotions.

When you do engage them, use an active listening approach to defuse tension. First, validate their emotions and feelings. Next, affirm them as a person of faith in Christ and a beloved child. Finally, offer an opportunity for reconciliation by providing grace to find a point of common ground to restore harmony. With time, you will learn to respond rather than simply react with anger and offense in these situations.

Overcoming stigma. Stigma is always born out of fear and misinformation and can only be overcome by honesty and education. The purpose of stigma is to minimize, disgrace, or dehumanize someone so that inaction and a lack of compassion can be justified. Others' wrongly held views and beliefs (stigma) are hurtful and not the child's fault; don't own them. Mental disorders are not the result of personal sin, generational sin, weak faith, or demonic oppression or possession. All believers struggle with sin and weakness of faith at times, but God still chooses to love and care for us. Educate family and friends about the causes and treatments of the child's mental disorder. Find a supportive faith community where the family and child are safe to recover rather than be condemned.

Opportunities to serve. When we serve others, we are actually serving God, "Then the King will say, 'I'm telling the solemn truth: Whenever you did one of these things to someone overlooked or ignored, that was me—you did it to me'" (Matthew 25:40 *The Message*). We are most like Jesus when we're serving others. After washing his disciples' feet, Jesus said, "I have given you an example to follow. Do as I have done to you" (John 13:14-15 NLT).

As the child gains stability, look for simple ways for them to serve and bless others. Whether at home, for a neighbor, or at church, serving provides a healthy way to look beyond personal difficulties and engage others with compassion. Serving others builds value and worth.

My hope is that this chapter has shown you that a comprehensive holistic mental-health-care plan is far more complex than simply taking pills and attending intermittent therapy sessions. A holistic mental-health-care plan offers children struggling with a mental disorder and their families a more complete framework for recovery. Recovery is a process, and in that process every aspect of a child's being must be taken into account for healing to be successful. For a detailed holistic mental-health recovery curriculum, please contact the Hope and Healing Center & Institute (mentalhealthgateway.org).

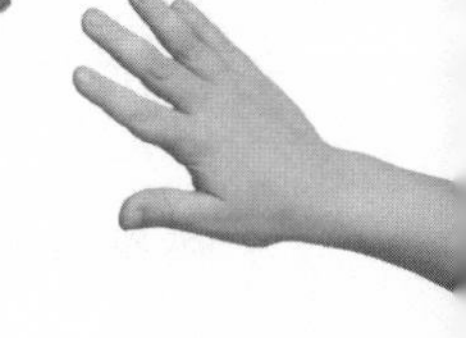

14

A Divine Opportunity

So then, while we have opportunity, let us do good to all people, and especially to those who are of the household of the faith.

GALATIANS 6:10

RESEARCH SHOWS that individuals struggling with mental-health problems are more likely to see a pastor before they engage a mental-health-care provider or physician.[1] A survey of church leaders by author and mental-health advocate Amy Simpson found that 44.5 percent of pastors report being approached two to five times a year for help with mental illness, while 32.8 percent report being approached six or more times.[2] My own research has shown that a majority of youth and college pastors report they are regularly ministering to multiple adolescents and young adults with serious mental-health problems such as depression and eating disorders.[3]

Viewed through the eyes of faith, the fact that those struggling with mental-health problems and their families are seeking assistance from the church first is a divine opportunity. God is sending those broken by mental illness to us so they might receive hope and healing. Given that 450 million individuals in the world are presently struggling with a mental-health problem, it is time for the church to recognize its role in what may be the great mission field of the twenty-first century.[4]

WHY THE CHURCH IS IMPORTANT

Our present mental-health-care system is not a true system of care. Rather, it is a confusing set of loosely associated resources that individuals and families find difficult to access or afford. While our existing mental-health resources are critically important, on their own, they do not provide a holistic approach to meeting the needs of children and adolescents struggling with mental illness. In addition, many children who would benefit from professional care do not receive it, largely because their families are unable to find an open door to the mental-health-care system. The body of Christ can offer the mental-health-care system four things it presently lacks: (1) hope that transcends circumstances, (2) a holistic view of humanity, (3) accessibility, and (4) supportive community.

Hope is the fuel that drives the engine of mental-health recovery. As long as one has hope, there is motivation and opportunity for change. Historically, severe mental illness has been conceptualized as a chronic medical condition in which stability is the best possible outcome for treatment. The hope presently offered by the mental-health-care system is symptom management. The church, however, understands that hope is more than a feeling; hope is a person, Jesus Christ. Hope in Christ transcends circumstances and sustains us when the world around us sees the situation as hopeless.

Second, the child struggling with a mental-health problem needs a holistic approach to treatment that takes into account all aspects of their being: physical, mental, spiritual, and relational. Treatments and interventions that focus solely on a single aspect of a person's being can bring limited relief at best. Specifically, medication alone is not as effective as medication in combination with therapy, support, and a healthy lifestyle. A holistic mental-health approach, however, is comprehensive, addressing the whole individual. The church's holistic view of humanity offers those struggling with a mental-health problem a more complete framework for recovery.

Third, accessibility is perhaps the biggest problem with our present system, but imagine what would happen if churches were equipped to effectively serve as front doors to mental-health care. Individuals in psychological distress who seek assistance from the church would be quickly identified and referred for professional care. What if churches were equipped not only to be effective front doors but also places where peer-led mental-health services were available onsite? These services would not replace professional mental-health care, but instead they would serve as an adjunct to those resources. Basic helpful interventions, such as psychoeducation and support groups, are ideal for implementation in a church setting. Services such as these, led by nonprofessionals, have been shown to be effective in managing symptoms and maintaining stability and have the added benefits of minimal cost and maximum accessibility.

Finally, a supportive community is a necessary factor in successful mental-health recovery. Grace-filled churches offer children and their families an accepting and supportive environment in which they can pursue healing and wholeness. The call of the church is to love one another; this offers the afflicted and their families a community of care and respite away from the struggles associated with mental-health problems. Ideally, the church, functioning in the power and grace of Christ, provides a safe place for the wounded to rest and recover.

WE ARE MISSING IT!

While research finds that individuals (and their families) struggling with mental illness are coming to the church for help, those same studies show that the church is mostly apathetic about mental-health issues. A vast majority of pastors report they rarely or never give sermons related to mental illness. A quarter of pastors say they are reluctant to get involved with those diagnosed with a mental disorder because of the time and resources required. Thus, few churches offer any mental-health related programs or services.[5]

More disturbing perhaps is that the Christian community is overspiritualizing mental-health problems in a large number of cases. In surveys of Christians diagnosed with a mental disorder who approached their church for assistance, 30-40 percent report that their mental illness was denied or dismissed. When the existence of mental illness was denied by the church, the individual's psychological distress was most commonly attributed to personal sin, weak faith, or the demonic. As might be expected, more than a quarter of these individuals report that the church's involvement made the matter worse and damaged their faith.[6]

As a community of believers, we must not withdraw from the problem of mental disorders but instead choose to face it with God's grace and wisdom. Our children and youth are struggling, and we, the followers of Jesus, have adopted a cold, judgmental approach to dealing with these problems. This is not who we are! Christ said that the world would know we were his disciples because of our love for one another (John 13:35). Where better for children, whether they have a mental disorder or not, to look for love and acceptance than the church? Where better for parents to go for support and comfort than the body of Christ? As a community, our approach to these problems should be one of love and grace. We must lead by example. So let us love one another, because love is from God (1 John 4:7).

EQUIPPING THE CHURCH

Every church is different; each has a specific set of needs and available resources. For the church to transform the mental-health-care system, it is not necessary for every congregation to be involved at the same level. It is only necessary that each congregation become involved. The following are suggestions of how churches might become more equipped to serve children and adolescents struggling with mental-health problems.

Mental-health training. Research shows that over 70 percent of pastors report feeling inadequately trained to recognize mental illness.[7] If all churches would simply train their staff to be able to recognize the signs and symptoms of mental illness, then pastors would become effective mental-health gatekeepers and access to the system would be increased. A number of organizations (e.g., National Alliance for the Mentally Ill, Mental Health America) offer mental-health training that pastors and their ministry staff can easily access.

Collaborative professional relationships. It is imperative that clergy build professional relationships with mental-health-care providers in their local community. Referrals to a professional one has a relationship with are more meaningful to the person being referred. A referral should not be seen as passing the buck but rather as a collaborative opportunity in which the pastor and mental-health provider work as a team to care for and support the struggling family. Clergy should vet a wide range of mental-health professionals in the community as potential referrals, including psychiatrists, clinical psychologists, clinical social workers, and counselors. The pastor should seek mental-health providers who are willing to work collaboratively on cases and who are affirming of the Christian faith.

Congregational education and awareness. Stigma and shame are barriers that keep a suffering child and family from receiving the care and support they need to recover. It is the responsibility of the clergy and ministry staff to educate their congregation that the church is a safe place to discuss our problems, including mental illness. This can be done in a number of ways. Place brochures, information regarding mental illness, and other available resources in the church entry or main office. Invite a local mental-health professional to speak or offer a seminar on mental illness.

Perhaps even more importantly the congregation must be educated about the process the church has put in place to care and support those who are struggling with mental-health problems. Do not assume that they know. A recent LifeWay Research study found that while 68 percent of pastors reported that their church kept a list of local mental-health referrals for members, only 28 percent of their congregants reported knowing about it.[8]

Pastoral care team. All followers of Christ are called to "bear one another's burdens" (Galatians 6:2). The care and support of those who are struggling is not just the responsibility of a few hired clergy but the congregation as a whole. Establish and develop a pastoral care team or ministry within your church. Within your congregation God has placed individuals who are supernaturally gifted in mercy. Seek them out. Also recruit individuals with personal experiences to offer counsel in areas such as marriage, parenting, addiction, or divorce. A strong pastoral care ministry is vital when ministering to families struggling with mental-health problems.

Support groups. There is strong evidence for the clinical efficacy of peer-led support groups in mental-health recovery. It requires few resources for the church to allow organizations that offer mental-health support groups (e.g., National Alliance for the Mentally Ill, Depression and Bipolar Support Alliance, and Alcoholics Anonymous) to use the church's facility to hold regular weekly meetings. If the faith community is interested in being more directly involved in the delivery of support groups, partner with faith-based organizations such as Grace Alliance (mentalhealthgracealliance.org) or Fresh Hope (freshhope.us) to have congregants trained to lead groups. Support groups are highly beneficial to the caregivers of children and adolescents living with mental illness.

Sunday service. Breaking the silence is the first step in developing an environment that promotes hope and healing in those families living with mental illness. The weekly corporate gathering of the congregation is a great place to begin. As a faith community, pray in a general way each week for anyone who is struggling with a mental or emotional disorder. If your church has a time of prayer at the end of the service, explicitly invite individuals and families with mental-health problems to come forward for prayer. Prepare sermons that acknowledge the struggle experienced by those with mental illness; consider inviting a member of the church who has struggled with mental illness to share their story with the congregation during the service.

Sunday school. From day one, children's ministry leaders should create a partnership with parents to work toward assisting the afflicted child and family. At the first meeting, parents should be asked, What are your child's special needs or disabilities? How can we engage and support your child? Parents can then share tips, tactics, and strategies that work at home and in school. These can then be incorporated into the child's Sunday morning classroom experience.

Many churches offer a buddy system. Older students in the youth group, college students, or church members are recruited to serve as buddies (one-on-one support) during the Sunday school time. A buddy offers the support necessary for a child or adolescent living with a mental-health problem the opportunity to participate in the church's mainstream children's programs. This is a more inclusive approach than relocating everyone with special needs to a separate classroom or expecting the family to offer support to the child during Sunday school.

LITTLE ACTS OF GRACE

What would happen if a member of your congregation discovered someone in the church had cancer and needed assistance? What if a family lost a member through death or gained a member through birth? What if an individual suddenly lost their job or a couple was struggling with marital problems? These are everyday occurrences in the body of Christ, and believers are usually eager to get involved and help. What if a member of your congregation found out that a family in the church was struggling to care for a mentally ill child? Would they help? For good reason, mental illness is called the "no casserole illness." It is the church leader's job to empower their congregants to show grace in little ways.

Think about everything you do on a normal day. If your day is anything like mine, you must do a number of necessary tasks throughout the day, and a number of people (e.g., spouse, children, coworkers) are counting on you to do them or else everything comes to a grinding halt. People caring for a child with a mental disorder are no different. They also have lives and responsibilities. But because of their child's illness, they may be functioning at a level well below normal. Imagine how much chaos a mental disorder brings into a family. I'm talking about everyday things we can all relate to, things we can all help with. Mundane things like grocery shopping, picking kids up from school, preparing a meal, mowing the grass, going to the post office, and so on. Let me assure you, little acts of grace matter, and God will powerfully use them.

CONCLUSION

I hope the practical suggestions in this chapter will assist you in making your faith community a place of rest for children and families suffering from mental illness. By leading to the church those broken by mental-health problems, God has provided us with an opportunity to transform lives and impact our community and culture with the power of the gospel. It is time for the body of Christ to take the lead in combating this silent epidemic. May God's grace be our guide.

Faith, hope, and love: often that's all we have left. Watching your child suffer with a mental illness strips you of everything. You're left feeling empty, powerless, and confused. Even when all seems lost, there is still faith, hope, and love. Faith in a caring, all powerful Creator. Hope that he is faithfully working in the midst of your trails. His unconditional love that sustains your life and quiets your fears. I hope this book has better educated you about children's mental disorders and shown you that God is present in their lives and yours. The journey that the care provider is on is overwhelming, but that's okay because God has overcome the world (John 16:33). Mental disorders do not have the final word, "we *are* afflicted in every way, but not crushed; perplexed, but not despairing; persecuted, but not forsaken; struck down, but not destroyed" (2 Corinthians 4:8-9). Jesus doesn't expect us to be able to handle these situations on our own. He wants to walk through it with us, empowering us with his Spirit so that we can do the impossible for our children. Hold onto faith, trust his promises, and rest in his love.

Notes

1 A GIFT AND A REWARD

[1]Matthew S. Stanford and Kandice McAlister, "Perceptions of Serious Mental Illness in the Local Church," *Journal of Religion, Disability and Health* 12 (2008): 144-53; Matthew S. Stanford, "Demon or Disorder: A Survey of Attitudes Toward Mental Illness in the Christian Church," *Mental Health, Religion and Culture* 10 (2007): 445-49.

[2]Mariam Arain et al., "Maturation of the Adolescent Brain," *Neuropsychiatric Disease and Treatment* 9 (2013): 449-61; Elizabeth R. Sowell et al., "Mapping Cortical Change Across the Human Life Span," *Nature Neuroscience* 6 (2003): 309-15.

[3]Original sin is the innate tendency to sin (sinful nature) that all human beings have inherited from Adam as a result of the fall.

2 DIAGNOSIS AND TREATMENT

[1]Andres De Los Reyes and Alan E. Kazdin, "Informant Discrepancies in the Assessment of Childhood Psychopathology: A Critical Review, Theoretical Framework, and Recommendations for Further Study," *Psychological Bulletin* 131 (2005): 483-509; Thomas M. Achenbach et al., "Child/Adolescent Behavioral and Emotional Problems: Implications of Cross-Informant Correlations for Situational Specificity," *Psychological Bulletin* 101 (1987): 213-32.

[2]Centers for Disease Control and Prevention, "Mental-Health Surveillance Among Children—United States, 2005-2011," *Morbidity and Mortality Weekly Report* 62 (2013): 1-35.

[3]Ronald C. Kessler et al., "Age of Onset of Mental Disorders: A Review of Recent Literature," *Current Opinion in Psychiatry* 20 (2007): 359-64.

[4]Melonie Heron, "Deaths: Leading Causes for 2014," *National Vital Statistics Reports* 65 (2016): 1-95.

[5]"National Survey Tracks Rates of Common Mental Disorders Among American Youth," National Institutes of Health, December 14, 2009, www.nih.gov/news-events/news-releases/national-survey-tracks-rates-common-mental-disorders-among-american-youth.

[6]National Mental Health Advisory Council, "Health Care Reform for Americans with Severe Mental Illnesses," *American Journal of Psychiatry* 150 (1993): 1450-52.

[7]"SAMHSA's Working Definition of Recovery: 10 Guiding Principles of Recovery," Substance Abuse and Mental Health Administration, 2012, https://store.samhsa.gov/product/SAMHSA-s-Working-Definition-of-Recovery/PEP12-RECDEF.

[8]"Treatment of Children with Mental Illness: Frequently Asked Questions About the Treatment of Mental Illness in Children," National Institute of Mental Health, NIH Publication no. 09-4702 (2009).

3 QUESTIONS AND ANSWERS

[1]Harvey A. Whiteford et al., "Estimating Remission from Untreated Major Depression: A Systematic Review and Meta-Analysis," *Psychological Medicine* 43 (2013): 1569-85; John R. Weisz et al., "Effects of Psychotherapy with Children and Adolescents Revisited: A Meta-Analysis of Treatment Outcome Studies," *Psychological Bulletin* 117 (1995): 450-68; John R. Weisz et al., "Effectiveness of Psychotherapy with Children and Adolescents: A Meta-Analysis for Clinicians," *Journal of Consulting and Clinical Psychology* 55 (1987): 542-49.

[2]Ming T. Tsuang et al., "Gene-Environment Interactions in Mental Disorders," *World Psychiatry* 3 (2004): 73-83.

[3]Izyaslav Lapin, "Phenibut (beta-phenyl-GABA): A Tranquilizer and Nootropic Drug," *CNS Drug Review* 7 (2001): 471-81.

[4]William F. Byerley et al., "5-Hydroxytryptophan: A Review of Its Antidepressant Efficacy and Adverse Effects," *Journal of Clinical Psychopharmacology* 7 (1987):127-37.

[5]Marlene P. Freeman et al., "Omega-3 Fatty Acids: Evidence Basis for Treatment and Future Research in Psychiatry," *Journal of Clinical Psychiatry* 67 (2006): 1954-67.

4 DIFFERENT: AUTISM SPECTRUM DISORDER

[1]Advocates for individuals with intellectual disability rightfully assert that the term *mental retardation* has negative connotations, has become offensive to many people, and often results in misunderstandings about the nature of the disorder and those who have it. In October 2010, Congress passed Rosa's Law, which changed references to "mental retardation" in specified Federal laws to "intellectual disability," and references to "a mentally retarded individual" to "an individual with an intellectual disability." This change in terminology is reflected in the DSM-5.

[2]Chris Plauché Johnson, "Early Clinical Characteristics of Children with Autism," in *Autistic Spectrum Disorders in Children*, ed. V. B. Gupta (New York: Marcel Dekker, 2004), 85-123.

[3]This condition is called echolalia, the pathological repetition of what is said by other people as if echoing them.

[4]Eugen Bleuler, *Dementia Praecox, oder, Gruppe der Schizophrenien* (Leipzig: Franz Deuticke, 1911).

[5]Leo Kanner, "Autistic Disturbances of Affective Contact," *Nervous Child* 2 (1943): 217–50.

[6]The DSM-5 states, "Individuals with a well-established DSM-IV diagnosis of autistic disorder, Asperger's disorder, or pervasive developmental disorder not otherwise specified should be given the diagnosis of autism spectrum disorder."

[7]Other neurodevelopmental disorders include intellectual developmental disorder, language disorder, attention-deficit/hyperactivity disorder, specific learning disorder, and tic disorders.

[8]Nicolas A. Crossley et al., "Neuroimaging Distinction Between Neurological and Psychiatric Disorders," *British Journal of Psychiatry* 207 (2015): 429-34.

[9]Mayada Elsabbagh et al., "Global Prevalence of Autism and Other Pervasive Developmental Disorders," *Autism Research* 5 (2012): 160-79.

[10]Deborah L. Christensen et al., "Prevalence and Characteristics of Autism Spectrum Disorder Among Children Aged 8 Years—Autism and Developmental Disabilities Monitoring Network, 11 Sites, United States, 2012," *Surveillance Summaries* 65 (2016): 1-23.

[11]Simon Baron-Cohen et al., "Prevalence of Autism-Spectrum Conditions: UK School-Based Population Study," *British Journal of Psychiatry* 194 (2009): 500-509.

[12]"Research on Autism Spectrum Disorder," Centers for Disease Control and Prevention, accessed April 2, 2019, www.cdc.gov/ncbddd/autism/research.html.

[13]Jessica Wright, "Autism Rates in the United States Explained," *Spectrum*, March 2, 2017, https://spectrumnews.org/news/autism-rates-united-states-explained.

[14]Shafali Spurling Jeste and Roberto Tuchman, "Autism Spectrum Disorder and Epilepsy: Two Sides of the Same Coin?" *Journal of Child Neurology* 30 (2015): 1963-71.

[15]Emma W. Viscidi et al., "Clinical Characteristics of Children with Autism Spectrum Disorder and Co-Occurring Epilepsy," *PLOS One* 8 (2013): https://doi.org/10.1371/journal.pone.0067797.

[16]Claire Amiet et al., "Epilepsy in Autism Is Associated with Intellectual Disability and Gender: Evidence from Meta-Analysis," *Biological Psychiatry* 64 (2008): 577-82.

[17]Jon Baio et al., "Prevalence of Autism Spectrum Disorder Among Children Aged 8 Years—Autism and Developmental Disabilities Monitoring Network, 11 Sites, United States, 2010," *Surveillance Summaries* 63 (2014): 1-21.

[18]Laura A. Schieve et al., "Concurrent Medical Conditions and Health Care Use and Needs Among Children with Learning and Behavioral Developmental Disabilities, National Health Interview Survey, 2006–2010," *Research in Developmental Disabilities* 33 (2012): 467-76.

[19]Michaeline Bresnahan et al., "Association of Maternal Report of Infant and Toddler Gastrointestinal Symptoms with Autism: Evidence from a Prospective Birth Cohort," *JAMA Psychiatry* 72 (2015): 466-74.

[20]Cecilia Belardinelli et al., "Comorbid Behavioral Problems and Psychiatric Disorders in Autism Spectrum Disorders," *Journal of Childhood and Developmental Disorders* 2 (2016): https://doi.org/10.4172/2472-1786.100019.

[21]Valproic acid is an anticonvulsant used to treat certain types of seizures (epilepsy), the manic phase of bipolar disorder, and migraine headaches. Jakob Christensen et al., "Prenatal Valproate Exposure and Risk of Autism Spectrum Disorders and Childhood Autism," *Journal of the American Medical Association* 309 (2013): 1696-703; Paula Krakowiak et al., "Maternal Metabolic Conditions and Risk for Autism and Other Neurodevelopmental Disorders," *Pediatrics* 129 (2012): e1121-8.

[22]Maureen S. Durkin et al., "Advanced Parental Age and the Risk of Autism Spectrum Disorder," *American Journal of Epidemiology* 168 (2008): 1268-76; David Cohen et al., "Specific Genetic Disorders and Autism: Clinical Contribution Towards Their Identification," *Journal of Autism and Developmental Disorders* 35 (2005): 103-16.

[23]Sven Sandin et al., "The Heritability of Autism Spectrum Disorder," *Journal of the American Medical Association* 318 (2017): 1182-84.

[24]Sven Sandin et al., "The Familial Risk of Autism," *Journal of the American Medical Association* 311 (2014): 1170-77.

[25]Antonio Y. Hardan et al., "Brain Volume in Autism," *Journal of Child Neurology* 2001 (16): 421-24.

[26]Cortical dysgenesis describes a wide spectrum of brain anomalies that involve abnormal development of the cerebral cortex. Christine Ecker et al., "Describing the Brain in Autism in Five Dimensions—Magnetic

Resonance Imaging-Assisted Diagnosis of Autism Spectrum Disorder Using a Multiparameter Classification Approach," *Journal of Neuroscience* 30 (2010): 10612-623; David G. Amaral et al., "Neuroanatomy of Autism," *Trends in Neuroscience* 31 (2008): 137-45.

[27]Chemically serotonin is 5-hydroxytryptophan, which is abbreviated 5-HT.

[28]Diane C. Chugani et al., "Developmental Changes in Brain Serotonin Synthesis Capacity in Autistic and Nonautistic Children," *Annals of Neurology* 45 (1999): 287-95.

[29]Monique Ernst et al., "Low Medial Prefrontal Dopaminergic Activity in Autistic Children," *Lancet* 350 (1997): 638.

[30]Diane C. Chugani, "Neuroimaging and Neurochemistry of Autism," *Pediatric Clinics of North America* 59 (2012): 63-73.

[31]Javier Virues-Ortega, "Applied Behavior Analytic Intervention for Autism in Early Childhood: Meta-Analysis, Meta-Regression and Dose-Response Meta-Analysis of Multiple Outcomes," *Clinical Psychology Review* 30 (2010): 387-99.

[32]In the first century it was commonly believed that individuals with seizures were maddened by Selene, the goddess of the moon, or affected by the phases of the moon, thus they were referred to as moonstruck. In Latin "moonstruck" is translated as *lunatic*.

5 DISTRACTED: ATTENTION-DEFICIT HYPERACTIVITY DISORDER

[1]American Psychiatric Association, *Diagnostic and Statistical Manual of Mental Disorders*, 5th ed. (Washington, DC: American Psychiatric Association, 2013). Hereafter *Diagnostic and Statistical Manual of Mental Disorders* will be shortened to DSM followed by the edition.

[2]DSM-5, 61.

[3]DSM-5, 61.

[4]DSM-5, 61.

[5]George F. Still, "Some Abnormal Psychical Conditions in Children," *Lancet* 1 (1902): 1008-12.

[6]DSM-IV-TR, 87.

[7]Melissa L. Danielson et al., "Prevalence of Parent-Reported ADHD Diagnosis and Associated Treatment Among U.S. Children and Adolescents, 2016," *Journal of Child Clinical & Adolescent Psychology* (2018): https://doi.org/10.1080/15374416.2017.1417860.

[8]Patricia N. Pastor, et al., "Association Between Diagnosed ADHD and Selected Characteristics Among Children Aged 4-17 Years: United States, 2011–2013," *NCHS Data Brief*, 201 (2015), https://nchstats.com/2015/05/14/association-between-diagnosed-adhd-and-selected-characteristics-among-children-aged-4-17-years-united-states-2011-2013.

[9]Tanya E. Froehlich, et al., "Update on Environmental Risk Factors for Attention-Deficit/Hyperactivity Disorder," *Current Psychiatry Report*, 13 (2011): 333-44.

[10]Cedric Galera et al., "Early Risk Factors for Hyperactivity-Impulsivity and Inattention Trajectories from Age 17 Months to 8 Years," *Archives of General Psychiatry* 68 (2011): 1267-75; Kati Heinonen et al., "Behavioural Symptoms of Attention Deficit/Hyperactivity Disorder in Preterm and Term Children Born Small and Appropriate for Gestational Age: A Longitudinal Study," *BMC Pediatrics* 10 (2010): 91; Tanya E. Froehlich et al., "Association of Tobacco and Lead Exposures with Attention-Deficit/Hyperactivity Disorder," *Pediatrics* 124 (2009): e1054-e1063.

[11]Laura J. Stevens et al., "Dietary Sensitivities and ADHD Symptoms: Thirty-five Years of Research," *Clinical Pediatrics* 50 (2011): 279-93.

[12]Lily Hechtman et al., "Families of Children with Attention Deficit Hyperactivity Disorder: A Review," *Canadian Journal of Psychiatry* 41 (1996): 350-60.

[13]Russell A. Barkley, "Behavioral Inhibition, Sustained Attention, and Executive Functions: Constructing a Unifying Theory of ADHD," *Psychological Bulletin* 121 (1997): 65-94.

[14]Robert J. Barry et al., "A Review of Electrophysiology in Attention-Deficit/Hyperactivity Disorder: I. Qualitative and Quantitative Electroencephalography," *Clinical Neurophysiology* 114 (2003): 171-83.

[15]Gianfranco Spalletta et al., "Prefrontal Blood Flow Dysregulation in Drug Naive ADHD Children Without Structural Abnormalities," *Journal of Neural Transmission* 108 (2001): 1203-16; Daniel G. Amen and Blake D. Carmichael, "High-Resolution Brain SPECT Imaging in ADHD," *Annals of Clinical Psychiatry* 9 (1997): 81-6.

[16]F. Xavier Catellanos et al., "Developmental Trajectories of Brain Volume Abnormalities in Children and Adolescents with Attention-Deficit/Hyperactivity Disorder," *Journal of the American Medical Association* 288 (2002): 1740-48.

[17]Bertha K. Madras, Gregory M. Miller, and Alan J. Fischman, "The Dopamine Transporter and Attention-Deficit/ Hyperactivity Disorder," *Biological Psychiatry* 57 (2005): 1397-1409.

[18]James M. Swanson et al., "Dopamine Genes and ADHD," *Neuroscience and Biobehavioral Reviews* 24 (2000): 21-25.

[19]"Overview," CHADD, accessed April 2, 2019, https://chadd.org/for-parents/overview.

[20]Jose Martinez-Badia and Jose Martinez-Raga, "Who Says This Is a Modern Disorder? The Early History of Attention Deficit Hyperactivity Disorder," *World Journal of Psychiatry* 5 (2015): 379-386; Eugene Merzon et al., "Psychohistory: What Can We Learn About ADHD from the Old Testament," *Attention Deficit Hyperactivity Disorder* 7 (2015): S111-S112.

[21]Flavius Josephus, *The New Complete Works of Josephus*, trans. William Whiston (Grand Rapids: Kregel, 1999); the Midrash is an ancient rabbinic commentary on part of the Hebrew Scriptures. The earliest Midrashim come from the second century AD, although much of their content is older.

[22]Josephus, *Jewish Antiquities* 1.18.1.

[23]Josephus, *Jewish Antiquities* 2.1.1.

6 DEFIANT: DISRUPTIVE BEHAVIOR DISORDERS

[1]Jantiene Schoorl et al., "Emotion Regulation Difficulties in Boys with Oppositional Defiant Disorder/Conduct Disorder and the Relation with Comorbid Autism Traits and Attention Deficit Traits," *PLoS One*, 11 (2016): e0159323.

[2]SAMHSA, "Interventions for Disruptive Behavior Disorders KIT: Characteristics and Needs of Children with Disruptive Behavior Disorders and Their Families," HHS Publication no. SMA-11-4634 (2011).

[3]Lean, also known as purple drank, purple lean, sizzurp, and dirty sprite, is an intoxicating drink made from mixing prescription cough syrup with codeine, Sprite, and Jolly Rancher candy.

[4]David Marcus, "Juvenile Delinquency in the Bible and the Ancient Near East," *JANES* 13 (1981): 31-52.

[5]Glen O. Gabbard, ed., *Treatments of Psychiatric Disorders*, 5th ed. (Washington, DC: American Psychiatric Association, 2014), 739-40.

[6]Glorisa Canino et al., "Does the Prevalence of CD and ODD Vary Across Cultures?" *Social Psychiatry and Psychiatric Epidemiology* 45 (2010): 695-704.

[7]Kathleen Latimer et al., "Disruptive Behaviour Disorders: A Systematic Review of Environmental Antenatal and Early Years Risk Factors," *Child: Care, Health, & Development* (2012): 611-28.

[8]Nora Kerekes et al., "Oppositional Defiant- and Conduct Disorder-Like Problems: Neurodevelopmental Predictors and Genetic Background in Boys and Girls, in a Nationwide Study," *PeerJ* 2 (2014): e359, http://doi 10.7717/peerj.359; Danielle M. Dick et al., "Understanding the Covariation Among Childhood Externalizing Symptoms: Genetic and Environmental Influences on Conduct Disorder, Attention Deficit Hyperactivity Disorder, and Oppositional Defiant Disorder Symptoms," *Journal of Abnormal Child Psychology* 33 (2005): 219-29; and Frederick L. Coolidge et al., "Heritability and Comorbidity of Attention Deficit Hyperactivity Disorder with Behavioral Disorders and Executive Function Deficits: A Preliminary Investigation," *Developmental Neuropsychology* 17 (2000): 273-87.

[9]Walter Matthys et al., "The Neurobiology of Oppositional Defiant Disorder and Conduct Disorder: Altered Functioning in Three Mental Domains," *Development and Psychopathology* 25 (2013): 193-207; and Jeffrey D. Burke et al., "Oppositional Defiant Disorder and Conduct Disorder: A Review of the Past 10 Years, Part II," *Journal of the American Academy of Child and Adolescent Psychiatry* 41 (2002): 1275-93.

[10]Markus J. Kruesi et al., "A 2-Year Prospective Follow-up Study of Children and Adolescents with Disruptive Behavior Disorders," *Archives of General Psychiatry* 49 (1992): 429-35; and Markus J. Kruesi et al., "Cerebrospinal Fluid Monoamine Metabolites, Aggression and Impulsivity in Disruptive Behavior Disorders of Children and Adolescents," *Archives of General Psychiatry* 47 (1990): 419-26.

[11]Stephanie H. Van Goozen et al., "Hypothalamic-Pituitary-Adrenal Axis and Autonomic Nervous System Activity in Disruptive Children and Matched Controls," *Journal of the American Academy of Child and Adolescent Psychiatry* 39 (2000): 1438-45; and Angela S. Scerbo and David L. Kolko, "Salivary Testosterone and Cortisol in Disruptive Children: Relationship to Aggressive, Hyperactive, and Internalizing Behavior," *Journal of the American Academy of Child and Adolescent Psychiatry* 33 (1994): 1174-84.

[12]The deuterocanonical books are a set of ancient texts that primarily describe events that took place in the period between the Old and New Testaments. These writings are considered part of the biblical canon by some Christian denominations. The word *deuterocanonical* means "second canon."

7 HOPELESS: DEPRESSIVE DISORDERS

[1]Dwight L. Evans et al., "Depression and Bipolar Disorder: Commission on Adolescent Depression and Bipolar Disorder," in *Treating and Preventing Adolescent Mental-Health Disorders: What We Know and What We Don't Know. A Research Agenda for Improving the Mental Health of Our Youth,* ed. Dwight L. Evans et al. (New York: Oxford University Press, 2005).

[2]Leon Cytryn and Donald H. McKnew, "Proposed Classification of Childhood Depression," *American Journal of Psychiatry* 129 (1972): 149-55.

[3]Kathleen Ries Merikangas et al., "Prevalence and Treatment of Mental Disorders Among US Children in the 2001–2004 NHANES," *Pediatrics* 125 (2010): 71-81; and Uma Rao and Li-Ann Chen, "Characteristics, Correlates, and Outcomes of Childhood and Adolescent Depressive Disorders," *Dialogues in Clinical Neuroscience* 11 (2009): 45-62.

[4]William E. Copeland et al., "Prevalence, Comorbidity, and Correlates of DSM-5 Proposed Disruptive Mood Dysregulation Disorder," *American Journal of Psychiatry* 170 (2013): 171-79; and DSM-5.

[5]Elizabeth C. Braithwaite et al., "Prenatal Risk Factors for Depression: A Critical Review of the Evidence and Potential Mechanisms," *Journal of Developmental Origins of Health and Disease* 5 (2014): 339-350.

[6]Anita Thapar et al., "Depression in Adolescence," *Lancet* 379 (2012): 1056-67.

[7]Ellen Leibenluft, "Severe Mood Dysregulation, Irritability, and the Diagnostic Boundaries of Bipolar Disorder in Youths," *American Journal of Psychiatry* 168 (2011): 129-42.

[8]Lisa M. Kentgen et al., "Electroencephalographic Asymmetries in Adolescents with Major Depression: Influence of Comorbidity with Anxiety Disorders," *Journal of Abnormal Psychology* 109 (2000): 797-802.

[9]The limbic system is a set of structures deep within the brain that controls our most basic emotions (e.g., fear, pleasure, and anger) and drives (e.g., hunger, sex, and care of offspring).

[10]Jillian L. Wiggins et al., "Neural Correlates of Irritability in Disruptive Mood Dysregulation and Bipolar Disorders," *American Journal of Psychiatry* 173 (2016): 722-30; Melissa A. Brotman et al., "Amygdala Activation During Emotion Processing of Neural Faces in Children with Severe Mood Dysregulation Versus ADHD or Bipolar Disorder," *American Journal of Psychiatry* 167 (2010): 61-69; and Isabelle M.

Rosso et al., "Amygdala and Hippocampus Volumes in Pediatric Major Depression," *Biological Psychiatry* 57 (2005): 21-26.

[11]Paul E. Croarkin et al., "Evidence for Increased Glutamatergic Cortical Facilitation in Children and Adolescents with Major Depressive Disorder," *Journal of the American Medical Association Psychiatry* 70 (2013): 291-99; and Vilma Gabbay et al., "Anterior Cingulated Cortex Gamma-Aminobutyric Acid in Depressed Adolescents," *Archives of General Psychiatry* 69 (2012): 139-49.

[12]Ghanshyam N. Pandey et al., "Higher Expression of Serotonin 5-HT_{2A} Receptors in the Postmortem Brains of Teenage Suicide Victims," *American Journal of Psychiatry* 159 (2002): 419-29.

[13]Nestor L. Lopez-Duran et al., "Hypothalamic–Pituitary–Adrenal Axis Dysregulation in Depressed Children and Adolescents: A Meta-Analysis," *Psychoneuroendocrinology* 34 (2009): 1272-83.

[14]Amy H. Cheung et al., "Pediatric Depression: An Evidence-Based Update on Treatment Interventions," *Current Psychiatry Reports* 15 (2013): 381-89.

[15]Craig J Whittington et al., "Selective Serotonin Reuptake Inhibitors in Childhood Depression: Systematic Review of Published Versus Unpublished Data," *The Lancet* 363 (2004): 1341-45.

[16]Daniel J. Reidenberg, "Suicide," in Handbook of Adolescent Behavioral Problems: Evidence-Based Approaches to Prevention and Treatment, ed. Thomas P. Gullotta et al., 2nd ed. (New York: Springer, 2015), 222.

[17]Leon Tourian et al., "Treatment Options for the Cardinal Symptoms of Disruptive Mood Dysregulation Disorder," *Journal of the Canadian Academy of Child and Adolescent Psychiatry* 24 (2015): 41-54.

[18]Asmodeus was considered to be an evil king of demon spirits, one of the seven princes of hell from the Greek or Persian times. He was the demon of lust who twisted sexual desires.

8 EMOTIONAL: BIPOLAR DISORDERS

[1]Dyslexia is difficulty in learning to read or interpret words, letters, and other symbols, while dysgraphia is a writing disorder associated with impaired handwriting.

[2]Jules Baillarger, "Notes sur un genre de folie don't les acce's sont caracte´rise´s par deux pe´riodes re´gulie'res, l'une de de´pression, l'autre d'excitation," *Bulletin de l Academie Nationale de Medecine (Paris)* 19 (1854): 340; and Jean-Pierre Falret, "Memoire sur la folie

circulaire," *Bulletin de l Academie Nationale de Medecine (Paris)* 19 (1854): 382-415.

[3]Emil Kraepelin, *Psychiatrie: Ein Lehrbuch für Studierende und Ärzte* (Leipzig: Ambrosius Barth, 1896).

[4]The term *manic-depressive illness* was changed to bipolar disorder primarily to help minimize the stigma associated with referring to individuals living with manic-depression as maniacs.

[5]Ira Glovinsky, "A Brief History of Childhood-Onset Bipolar Disorder Through 1980," *Child and Adolescent Psychiatric Clinics of North America* 11 (2002): 443-60.

[6]See chapter seven for a full description of disruptive mood dysregulation disorder.

[7]Kathleen Ries Merikangas et al., "Lifetime Prevalence of Mental Disorders in U.S. Adolescents: Results from the National Comorbidity Survey Replication—Adolescent Supplement (NCS-A)," *Journal of the American Academy of Child and Adolescent Psychiatry* 49 (2010): 980-89.

[8]Tobias A. Rowland and Steven Marwaha, "Epidemiology and Risk Factors for Bipolar Disorder," *Therapeutic Advances in Psychopharmacology* 8 (2018): 251-69.

[9]Mani N. Pavuluri et al., "Biological Risk Factors in Pediatric Bipolar Disorder," *Biological Psychiatry* 60 (2006): 936-41.

[10]Stephen V. Faraone, Stephen J. Glattbe, and Ming T. Tsuang, "The Genetics of Pediatric-Onset Bipolar Disorder," *Biological Psychiatry* 53 (2003): 970-77.

[11]Jack Edvardsen et al., "Heritability of Bipolar Spectrum Disorders. Unity or Heterogeneity?" *Journal of Affective Disorders* 106 (2008): 229-40; and Stephen V. Faraone et al., "The Genetics of Pediatric-Onset Bipolar Disorder," *Biological Psychiatry* 53 (2003): 970-77.

[12]Daniel P. Dickstein et al., "Frontotemporal Alterations in Pediatric Bipolar Disorder," *Archives of General Psychiatry* 62 (2005): 734-41; Jean A. Frazier et al., "Structural Brain Magnetic Resonance Imaging of Limbic and Thalamic Volumes in Pediatric Bipolar Disorder," *American Journal of Psychiatry* 162 (2005): 1256-65; Jean A. Frazier et al., "Cortical Gray Matter Differences Identified by Structural Magnetic Resonance Imaging in Pediatric Bipolar Disorder," *Bipolar Disorder* 7 (2005): 555-69; and Simerjit Kaur et al., "Cingulate Cortex Anatomical Abnormalities in Children and Adolescents with Bipolar Disorder," *American Journal of Psychiatry* 162 (2005): 1637-43.

[13]Andrea Spencer et al., "Glutamatergic Dysregulation in Pediatric Psychiatricdisorders: A Systematic Review of the Magnetic Resonance Spectroscopy Literature," *Journal of Clinical Psychiatry* 75 (2014): 1226-41.

[14]Constance M. Moore et al., "Mania, Glutamate/Glutamine and Risperidone in Pediatric Bipolar Disorder: A Proton Magnetic Resonance Spectroscopy Study of the Anterior Cingulate Cortex," *Journal of Affective Disorder* 99 (2007): 19-25.

[15]Sally M. Weinstein et al., "Psychosocial Interventions for Pediatric Bipolar Disorder (PBD): Current and Future Directions," *Expert Review of Neurotherapeutics* 13 (2013): 843-50.

[16]Tatiana L. Peruzzolo et al., "Pharmacotherapy of Bipolar Disorder in Children and Adolescents: An Update," *Revista Brasileira de Psiquiatria* 35 (2013): 393-405.

9 FEARFUL: ANXIETY DISORDERS

[1]DSM-5, 189.

[2]Marc-Antoine Crocq, "A History of Anxiety: From Hippocrates to DSM," *Dialogues in Clinical Neuroscience* 17 (2015): 319-25.

[3]DSM-5; K. Beesdo, S. Knappe, and D. S. Pine, "Anxiety and Anxiety Disorders in Children and Adolescents: Developmental Issues and Implications for DSM-V," *Psychiatric Clinics of North America* 32 (2009): 483-524.

[4]Jean M. Twenge, "The Age of Anxiety? Birth Cohort Change in Anxiety and Neuroticism, 1952–1993," *Journal of Personality and Social Psychology* 79 (2000): 1007-21.

[5]Rachel L. Grover, Golda S. Ginsburg, and Nick Ialongo, "Childhood Predictors of Anxiety Symptoms: A Longitudinal Study," *Child Psychiatry and Human Development* 36 (2005): 133-53.

[6]Katharina Domschke and Jürgen Deckert, "Genetics," in *Behavioral Neurobiology of Anxiety and Its Treatment*, ed. Murray B. Stein and Thomas Steckler (New York: Springer, 2010), 63-75.

[7]John Hettema et al., "A Review and Meta-Analysis of the Genetic Epidemiology of Anxiety Disorders," *American Journal of Psychiatry* 158 (2001):1568-78; and Wolfgang Maier et al., "A Controlled Family Study in Panic Disorder," *Journal of Psychiatric Research* 27 (1993): 79-87.

[8]Jennifer U. Blackford and Daniel S. Pine, "Neural Substrates of Childhood Anxiety Disorders: A Review of Neuroimaging Findings,"

Child and Adolescent Psychiatric Clinics of North America, 21 (2012): 501-25; and Eric B. McClure et al., "Abnormal Attention Modulation of Fear Circuit Function in Pediatric Generalized Anxiety Disorder," *Archives of General Psychiatry* 64 (2007): 97-106.

[9]Gilberto Gerra et al., "Neuroendocrine Responses to Psychological Stress in Adolescents with Anxiety Disorders," *Neuropsychobiology* 42 (2000): 82-92; Floyd R. Sallee et al., "Yohimbine Challenge in Children with Anxiety Disorders," *American Journal of Psychiatry* 157 (2000): 1236-42; and Floyd R. Sallee et al., "Clonidine Challenge in Childhood Anxiety Disorder," *Journal of the American Academy of Child and Adolescent Psychiatry* 37 (1998): 655-62.

[10]Anne Marie Albano and Philip C. Kendall, "Cognitive Behavioural Therapy for Children and Adolescents with Anxiety Disorders: Clinical Research Advances," *International Review of Psychiatry* 14 (2002): 129-34.

[11]Jeffrey R. Strawn et al., "Establishing the Neurobiological Basis of Treatment in Children and Adolescents with Generalized Anxiety Disorder," *Depression and Anxiety* 29 (2012): 328-39; and Ian Kodish et al., "Pharmacotherapy for Anxiety Disorders in Children and Adolescents," *Dialogues in Clinical Neuroscience* 13 (2011): 439-52.

10 WOUNDED: POSTTRAUMATIC STRESS DISORDER

[1]DSM-5.

[2]Nancy C. Andreasen, "Posttraumatic Stress Disorder: A History and a Critique," *Annals of the New York Academy of Science* 1208 (2010): 67-71.

[3]Benjamin E. Saunders and Zachary W. Adams, "Epidemiology of Traumatic Experiences in Childhood," *Child and Adolescent Psychiatric Clinics of North America* 23 (2014): 167-84.

[4]Kathleen Ries Merikangas et al., "Lifetime Prevalence of Mental Disorders in US Adolescents: Results from the National Comorbidity Study-Adolescent Supplement (NCS-A)," *Journal of the American Academy of Child and Adolescent Psychiatry* 49 (2010): 980-89.

[5]David Trickey et al., A Meta-Analysis of Risk Factors for Post-Traumatic Stress Disorder in Children and Adolescents," *Clinical Psychology Review* 32 (2012): 122-38.

[6]William H. Sack et al., "Posttraumatic Stress Disorder Across Two Generations of Cambodian Refugees," *Journal of the American Academy of Child and Adolescent Psychiatry* 34 (1995): 1160-66.

[7]Murray B. Stein et al., "Genetic and Environmental Influences on Trauma Exposure and Posttraumatic Stress Disorder Symptoms: A Twin Study," *American Journal of Psychiatry* 159 (2002): 1675-81; and William R. True et al., "A Twin Study of Genetic and Environmental Contributions to Liability for Posttraumatic Stress Symptoms," *Archives of General Psychiatry* 50 (1993): 257-64.

[8]Ana Carolina C. Milani, et al., "Does Pediatric Post-Traumatic Stress Disorder Alter the Brain? Systematic Review and Meta-Analysis of Structural and Functional Magnetic Resonance Imaging Studies," *Psychiatry and Clinical Neurosciences* 71 (2017): 154-69; Michael D. De Bellis et al., "Brain Structures in Pediatric Maltreatment-Related Posttraumatic Stress Disorder: A Sociodemographically Matched Study," *Biological Psychiatry* 52 (2002): 1006-78; and Victor G. Carrion et al., "Attenuation of Frontal Asymmetry in Pediatric Posttraumatic Stress Disorder," *Biological Psychiatry* 50 (2001): 943-51.

[9]Danya Glaser, "Child Abuse and Neglect and the Brain—A Review," *Journal of Child Psychology and Psychiatry* 41 (2000): 97-116; and Michael D. De Bellis and Lisa A. Thomas, "Biologic Findings of Post-Traumatic Stress Disorder and Child Maltreatment," *Current Psychiatry Reports* 5 (2003):108-17.

[10]Donna Gillies et al., "Psychological Therapies for the Treatment of Post-Traumatic Stress Disorder in Children and Adolescents (Review)," *Evidence-Based Child Health: A Cochrane Review Journal* 8 (2013): 1004-16.

[11]Jeffrey R. Strawn et al., "Psychopharmacological Treatment of Posttraumatic Stress Disorder in Children and Adolescents: A Review," *Journal of Clinical Psychiatry* 71 (2010): 932-41.

[12]Flavius Josephus, *The New Complete Works of Josephus*, trans. William Whiston (Grand Rapids: Kregel, 1999): 245-47.

11 CONSUMED: OBSESSIVE COMPULSIVE AND RELATED DISORDERS

[1]Jeremy Taylor, Ductor Dubitantium, or, The Rule of Conscience an All Her General Measures Serving as a Great Instrument for the Determination of Cases of Conscience: In Four Books (London: Printed by James Flesher for Richard Royston, 1660), 210.

[2]Neurosis is an antiquated term used to describe a relatively mild mental illness that is not caused by organic disease, involving symptoms of stress but not a loss of touch with reality.

[3]Michele Fornaro et al., "Obsessive-compulsive Disorder and Related Disorders: A Comprehensive Survey," *Annals of General Psychiatry* 8 (2009): 13; Sigmund Freud, "Notes on a Case of Obsessional Neurosis," (London, UK: Hogart Press, 1953) 151-318; Pierre Janet, "*Les Obsessions et la Psychathenie*," (Paris, France: Felix Alcan, 1903).

[4]"Hoarding Disorder," Mayo Clinic, accessed April 3, 2019, www.mayo clinic.org/diseases-conditions/hoarding-disorder/symptoms-causes /syc-20356056.

[5]Gustaf Brander et al., "Association of Perinatal Risk Factors with Obsessive-Compulsive Disorder: A Population-Based Birth Cohort, Sibling Control Study," *Journal of the American Medical Association* 73 (2016): 1135-44; and DSM-5.

[6]"Causes of OCD in Children," BeyondOCD.org, accessed April 3, 2019, http://beyondocd.org/information-for-parents/helping-a-child-who-has-ocd/causes-of-ocd-in-children.

[7]"Causes of OCD in Children."

[8]Heidi A. Browne et al., "Genetics of Obsessive-Compulsive Disorder and Related Disorders," *Psychiatric Clinics of North America* 37 (2014): 319-35; and Gregory L. Hanna et al., "A Family Study of Obsessive-Compulsive Disorder with Pediatric Probands," *American Journal of Medical Genetics* 134B (2005):13-19.

[9]Amitai Abramovitch et al., "Neuroimaging and Neuropsychological Findings in Pediatric Obsessive-Compulsive Disorder: A Review and Developmental Considerations," *Neuropsychiatry* 2 (2012): 313-29; and Frank P. MacMaster et al., "Brain Imaging in Pediatric Obsessive Compulsive Disorder," *Journal of the American Academy of Child and Adolescent Psychiatry* 47 (2008): 1262-72.

[10]Paul D. Arnold et al., "Association of a Glutamate (NMDA) Subunit Receptor Gene (GRIN2B) with Obsessive-Compulsive Disorder: A Preliminary Study," *Psychopharmacology* 174 (2004): 530-38; David R. Rosenberg et al., "Reduced Anterior Cingulated Glutamatergic Concentrations in Childhood OCD and Major Depression Versus Healthy Controls," *Journal of the American Academy of Child and Adolescent Psychiatry* 43 (2004): 1146-53; and David R. Rosenberg et al., "Decrease in Caudate Glutamatergic Concentrations in Pediatric Obsessive-Compulsive Disorder Patients Taking Paroxetine," *Journal of the American Academy of Child and Adolescent Psychiatry* 39 (2000): 1096-1103.

[11]Jonathan S. Abramowitz et al., "The Effectiveness of Treatment for Pediatric Obsessive-Compulsive Disorder: A Meta-Analysis," *Behavior Therapy* 36 (2005): 55-63.

[12]Edwards H. Reynolds and James V. Kinnier Wilson, "Neurology and Psychiatry in Babylon," *Brain* 137 (2014): 2611-19; and Bowden, Hugh, "Before Superstition and After: Theophrastus and Plutarch on Deisidaimonia," *Past & Present* 199 (2008): 56-71.

12 WORTHLESS: EATING DISORDERS

[1]Joseph A. Silverman, "Historical Development," in *Psychobiology and Treatment of Anorexia Nervosa and Bulimia Nervosa*, ed. Katherine A. Halmi (Washington, DC: American Psychiatric Press, 1992), 3-17.

[2]Albert J. Stunkard, "Eating Patterns and Obesity," *Psychiatric Quarterly* 33 (1959): 284-95.

[3]Sonja A. Swanson et al., "Prevalence and Correlates of Eating Disorders in Adolescents: Results from the National Comorbidity Survey Replication Adolescent Supplement," *Archives of General Psychiatry* 68 (2011): 714-23.

[4]Rebecka Peebles et al., "Self-Injury in Adolescents with Eating Disorders: Correlates and Provider Bias," *Journal of Adolescent Health* 48 (2011): 310-13.

[5]DSM-5; Christopher G. Fairburn, "Risk Factors for Anorexia Nervosa: Three Integrated Case-Control Comparisons," *Archives of Clinical Psychiatry* 56 (1999): 468-76; and Kathleen M. Pike and Judith Rodin, "Mothers, Daughters and Disordered Eating," *Journal of Abnormal Psychology* 100 (1991): 198-204.

[6]Laura M. Thornton et al., "The Heritability of Eating Disorders: Methods and Current Findings," *Current Topics in Behavioral Neuroscience* 6 (2011): 141-56.

[7]Frances Connan et al., "A Neurodevelopmental Model of Anorexia Nervosa," *Physiology & Behavior* 79 (2003): 13-24.

[8]Walter H. Kaye et al., "Anorexia and Bulimia Nervosa," *Annual Review of Medicine* 51 (2000): 299-313; and Guido K. Frank et al., "Reduced 5-HT2A Receptor Binding After Recovery from Anorexia Nervosa," *Biological Psychiatry* 52 (2002): 896-906.

[9]Alissa A. Haedt-Matt and Pamela K. Keel, "Revisiting the Affect Regulation Model of Binge Eating: A Meta-Analysis of Studies Using Ecological Momentary Assessment," *Psychological Bulletin* 137 (2011),

660-81; and Sarah E. Racine et al., "The Possible Influence of Impulsivity and Dietary Restraint on Associations Between Serotonin Genes and Binge Eating," *Journal of Psychiatric Research* 43 (2009): 1278-86.

[10]James Locke et al., "Treatment of Adolescent Eating Disorders: Progress and Challenges," *Minerva Psichiatrica* 51 (2010): 208-9.

[11]Kimberly A. Brownley et al., "Binge Eating Disorder Treatment: A Systematic Review of Randomized Controlled Trials," *International Journal of Eating Disorders* 40 (2007): 337-48.

[12]Gastroesophageal reflux is the result of acidic stomach contents regurgitating back into the esophagus.

[13]Judith would only eat "the day before the Sabbath, the Sabbath itself, the day before the new moon and the day of the new moon, and the festivals and days of rejoicing of the house of Israel" (Judith 8:6).

13 BEING HOLISTIC

[1]"Sleep and Mental-Health," *Harvard Mental Health Publishing*, updated March 18, 2019, www.health.harvard.edu/newsletter_article/Sleep-and-mental-health.

[2]Edward B. Rogers and Matthew S. Stanford, "A Church-Based Peer-Led Group Intervention for Mental Illness," *Mental Health, Religion, & Culture* 18 (2015): 470-81.

[3]Linda L. Barnes et al., "Spirituality, Religion, and Pediatrics: Intersecting Worlds of Healing," *Pediatrics* 106 (2000): 899-908.

[4]John W. Schoenheit, *The Christian's Hope: The Anchor of the Soul*, 2nd ed. (Indianapolis: Christian Educational Services, 2004), 5.

[5]John Piper, "What Is so Important About Christian Hope?" *Desiring God*, March 7, 2008, www.desiringgod.org/interviews/what-is-so-important-about-christian-hope.

14 A DIVINE OPPORTUNITY

[1]Philip S. Wang et al., "Patterns and Correlates of Contacting Clergy for Mental Disorders in the United States," *Health Services Research* 38 (2003): 647-73.

[2]Amy Simpson, *Troubled Minds: Mental Illness and the Church's Mission* (Downers Grove, IL: InterVarsity Press, 2013).

[3]William M. Hunter and Matthew S. Stanford, "Adolescent Mental Health: The Role of Youth and College Pastors," *Mental Health, Religion and Culture* 17 (2014): 957-66.

[4]"Mental Disorders Effect One in Four People," World Health Organization, October 4, 2001, www.who.int/whr/2001/media_centre/press_release/en.

[5]"Study of Acute Mental Illness and Christian Faith: Research Report," LifeWay Research, accessed April 5, 2019, http://lifewayresearch.com/mentalillnessstudy.

[6]Matthew S. Stanford and Kandace R. McAlister, "Perceptions of Serious Mental Illness in the Local Church," *Journal of Religion, Disability and Health* 12 (2008): 144-53; and Matthew S. Stanford, "Demon or Disorder: A Survey of Attitudes Toward Mental Illness in the Christian Church," *Mental Health, Religion and Culture* 10 (2007): 445-49.

[7]William M. Hunter and Matthew S. Stanford, "Adolescent Mental Health: The Role of Youth and College Pastors," *Mental Health, Religion and Culture* 17 (2014): 957-66; and Jennifer L. Farrell and Deborah A. Goebert, "Collaboration Between Psychiatrists and Clergy in Recognizing and treating Serious Mental Illness," *Psychiatric Services* 59 (2008): 437-40.

[8]"Study of Acute Mental Illness and Christian Faith."

Also by Matthew S. Stanford

978-0-8308-4507-0